The Physics of Business Growth

Ed Hess

The Physics of Business Growth

Mindsets, System, and Processes

Edward D. Hess and Jeanne Liedtka

An Imprint of Stanford University Press
Stanford, California

Stanford University Press
Stanford, California

Special discounts for bulk quantities of Stanford Briefs are available to corporations, professional associations, and other organizations. For details and discount information, contact the special sales department of Stanford University Press. Tel: (650) 736-1782, Fax: (650) 736-1784

Library of Congress Cataloging-in-Publication Data

Hess, Edward D., author.
  The physics of business growth : mindsets, system, and processes / Edward D. Hess and Jeanne Liedtka.
    pages cm
  Includes bibliographical references.
  ISBN 978-0-8047-8477-1 (pbk. : alk. paper)
  1. Corporations—Growth. 2. Industrial management. I. Liedtka, Jeanne, author. II. Title.
  HD2746.H467 2012
  657'.95—dc23   2012014466

Typeset by Classic Typography in 10.5/14 Bembo

*To our students, colleagues, executives, and consulting clients who have
made our work better and given us the opportunity to experiment and learn*

Contents

Preface

With *The Physics of Business Growth* we invite you to explore a nuanced and dynamic way to think about business growth and how it occurs. Many businesspeople think that the most critical element needed to grow a business is the right strategy. Our research and consulting experience has led us to conclude that the right strategy is not enough. To consistently grow you need much more. The "much more" is what this book is about.

The Physics of Business Growth presents a new formula for growth:

$$Growth = Mindsets + System + Processes$$

This Growth Formula is additive: consistent growth requires all three elements. Growth requires much more than a good strategy—it requires employees, managers, and leaders to have the right Growth Mindsets, the business to have the right growth environment created by an enabling internal Growth System, and the utilization of the right Growth Processes, which build upon strategic themes.

The second objective of this book is to engage you in learning and thinking deeply about Growth Mindsets, an internal Growth System, and Growth Processes. To engage you we will share with you our research and consulting findings through stories, cases, templates, and multiple tools that you can use in your business. Although almost all businesses strive to grow, our research shows that consistent business growth is the exception not the rule. We will share our learning from growth leaders and from exceptional, consistent growth companies. We strived to make this book a how-to book by presenting you not only with concepts and examples but also with tools to implement our findings.

Our third objective is to inspire you to think differently about growth and to act differently. Growth is not a linear process; rather, it is a continuous, iterative, proactive learning process involving critical inquiry, discovery, and experimentation mindsets, behaviors, and processes. It requires leaders of project teams, operating business units, and companies to think and behave in a manner that encourages Growth Mindsets and growth behaviors. Discovering, recognizing, and exploring growth opportunities requires a different way of thinking (mindset), different processes, and different organizational tolerances for risk and failures from those necessary for daily, 99-percent-defect-free business execution.

So, we invite you to join us in the exploration of *The Physics of Business Growth*.

Acknowledgments

Our research and this book have been generously funded by the Darden Foundation and the Batten Institute of the Darden Graduate School of Business at the University of Virginia. Thanks also to Amy Halliday and Katherine Ludwig for editing and production assistance; to Daniel Lombardi for cool design work; and to Margo Beth Fleming of Stanford University Press for her professionalism and Growth Mindset.

The Physics of Business Growth

1

Fighting the Physics of Growth

Ask managers at any level, in almost any organization, and they'll tell you that they struggle to produce the kind of profitable organic growth that investors demand. Consistently, organic growth is at the top of the list of challenges for business leaders—and at the top of their list of essential capabilities for ensuring success. And yet, there has been a surprising lack of attention to helping managers develop this ability. In fact, it is not even clear what the behaviors associated with successful growth leadership even *look like*—or what the organizational enablers of such behavior might be. That is why we have written this book.

For more than 15 years, we have been exploring—at first independently and recently together—how successful organic growth actually happens in organizations (see The Authors in back of book). Through our research and work with businesspeople, from frontline managers to CEOs, we've concluded that organizations are often their own worst enemy. They don't give managers and employees the tools to find growth; their business mindset and processes don't support people who do somehow stumble upon growth opportunities; and their corporate cultures, measurements, and rewards seal the deal by turning growth into an unnatural act.

People, process, culture, measurements, and rewards—all of these, as they exist in most organizations today, are at odds with what we think of as the "physics of growth." It is a physics that is radically different from the one we prepare managers to succeed in. Our aim here is to help you understand the difference between the physics of stability and the physics of growth, and to provide you with a map and a set of practical tools to navigate this brave new world.

What Do We Mean by the "Physics of Growth"?

After years of studying growth and working with managers at all levels trying to achieve it, we have come to believe that organic growth is, in fact, governed by its own *natural laws*, an underlying reality that sets the context for growth and innovation in much the same way that Einstein's law of relativity accounts for the movement of objects in the space-time continuum—or the way the underlying economics of an industry drives the success of business models. The most fundamental natural law of organic growth is that the only certainty is *un*certainty. The dominating forces are ambiguity and change; the processes at work involve exploration, invention, and experimentation. These elements, taken together, capture the distinct physics of organic growth.

Unfortunately, this physics is very different from the one that has long informed the design of business organizations; that physics is characterized by stability, predictability, and linearity. In both environments, people seek control over outcomes, but how they go about achieving that differs radically. Analysis, prediction, and rules usually work to achieve control in a stable, predictable environment where the process is geared for execution. But those approaches often backfire badly in the face of growth's uncertainty. Ignoring the physics of growth is like ignoring gravity: through sheer courage and herculean effort, managers can make things happen, but in doing so they continuously fight relentless forces that slow them down and sap their energy. Courageous and naturally growth-oriented leaders may still find a way to produce the growth they are asked to deliver (we've studied them and how they accomplish this)— but these managers tend to be few and do not a strategic capability make.

Many of the cultural values, systems, and processes in large organizations fight the physics of growth and its emphasis on exploration and invention rather than execution. The result is that growth leaders feel as if they are "swimming in molasses,"[1] as one manager described it. That is because even the best managed (perhaps *especially* the best managed) large organizations are beautifully designed to produce standardized, low-variance results through careful execution in an environment of predictability. They employ talented leaders at all levels who have learned (and may well be predisposed) to focus on efficiency and control. Because of this, they excel at execution—and at driving waste and variation out of the system—and they have a state-of-the-art tool kit for accomplishing this. Unfortunately, the pursuit of growth and innovation is inherently messy and inefficient. Unlike execution, exploration is a high-variance activity, and if, as work in the area of total quality management (TQM) would suggest, "variation is the mother of waste," it is also often the mother of invention.

The mindset, culture, and processes that drive successful execution in an existing business can, if unexamined, drive innovation into the ground, exhausting and discouraging the very people who are trying hardest to accomplish it, and killing inventive ideas before they see the light of day. Sporadic interventions and innovation consultants can help, as can people who courageously press on with innovation despite the odds. But these strategies work *in spite* of organizational forces, not because of them. Building a *strategic capability* for growth requires engaging the hearts and minds of employees at every level and giving them new tools to achieve a better balance between invention and execution. That's what this book is all about.

Learning from Las Vegas and Silicon Valley

You can learn a lot about the physics of growth by comparing who wins and loses in a Las Vegas casino. When it comes to growth, most managers, sadly, are like the little old lady with a cup of quarters playing the slots, just pulling the handle and hoping for the best. Sophisticated growth leaders—those who understand and leverage the physics of growth—are probably at the craps table. Craps is the preferred game of most professional gamblers (we are told) because it offers the most potential for making serious money—if you know how to play. It may *look* like the professional craps player is throwing the dice and hoping, just like the old lady at the slots, but there is a lot more going on. Discipline and focus, not luck, are the hallmarks of great craps players: they know how to manage the game in real time, assessing and sticking to what they can afford to lose, placing many bets, figuring out when to double down and when to get out, and staying alert to emerging opportunities and new developments. Sure, the odds are still in favor of the house; that is the reality of the game. But the chances of beating the odds are a lot higher at the craps table than they are at the slot machines.

Closer to home, this physics of growth is well understood by venture capitalists. VC firms' track records are not stellar: somewhere around two of every ten investments turn out to be winners. Do VCs consider themselves dismal failures? No, because they understand that the force at play here is uncertainty. And so they see themselves as managing *portfolios* of growth opportunities. Some of these will do well, but most, they realize, will not. They also know that their ability to predict at the early stages *which* two ventures will succeed is poor. They do not attribute this to their personal failings; instead, they recognize that the inability to predict is a property of the uncertainty surrounding any new business. Like professional gamblers, they develop a set of practices that acknowledge this reality: they bet heavily on the individual leader of a new business and look for people with experience (expecting both some successes and some failures in their background); they try to keep their bets small and affordable until they have better data; and they develop approaches that help them get in and out of new ventures intelligently and swiftly. Their goal, in other words, is to succeed—or fail fast and cheap.

When large organizations pursue growth, their mindsets are often completely out of sync with the reality that guides both craps players and VCs. Chances are that these organizations expect ten out of ten projects not only to win, but to win big. They demand that their managers and employees produce growth, inadvertently thwart their attempts, and uphold a system in which pulling the plug on a failed growth opportunity is a career-threatening act. Would-be growth leaders in this environment are like professional gamblers who are unable to act independently but instead receive instructions from on high—from a source that has little information about what is happening *this* minute in *this* particular game. Not a formula likely to win at craps—or in business.

What is behind this mismatch of expectations and realities? We believe it is a set of misconceptions about corporate growth. Let's look at what we know (or *think* we know) about how organizations achieve healthy growth.

Growth Myths

When it comes to growth, we have been taught the following "truths": Businesses either grow or die; all growth is good; growing bigger is always better; and public companies should grow in a linear manner as evidenced by ever-increasing quarterly earnings. Surprisingly, these beliefs have been embraced without rigorous analysis about how well they describe the actual growth trajectories of robust businesses. Nonetheless, they are the foundation of the short-term business mentality dominant in many C-suites, boardrooms, and Wall Street firms. And they are pure and simple fiction. These beliefs ignore the physics of growth. Businesses do not have to grow to stay alive; growth is not always good; bigger is not always better; and continuous linear growth is the rare exception, not the rule. Blindly following the dictates of these myths can drive bad corporate behaviors and inhibit real growth and innovation. It also can lead to artificially induced business volatility, lost opportunity, and premature destruction of businesses.

Yet, so powerful is the imperative for businesses to report growth that companies engage in a widely acknowledged "earnings game" to meet short-term projections instead of focusing on the hard work of managing portfolios of organic growth opportunities. This game takes the form of the "creation" of earnings through accounting elections, valuations, reserves, liberalizing credit policies, channel stuffing, deferring needed expenditures, selling assets, and myriad structured financial transactions. These non-authentic earnings are too often generated solely to meet Wall Street's growth and earnings demands.

You don't have to look far to see the downside of those demands: shareholder value squandered on overpriced and inappropriate acquisitions, managers chasing the wrong customers or cutting corners to meet inflated forecasts, CEOs with solid strategies hung out to dry for missing EPS projections by pennies. To satisfy Wall Street's obsession with growth, businesses are encouraged to make imprudent decisions that can harm their fundamentals in the long term. And, in some cases, those decisions simply camouflage a business's poor performance and underlying weaknesses. What is clear is that at its best, this earnings game makes it difficult for investors to assess the underlying strength of a business; at its worst, it incentivizes short-term profits to the detriment of a business's long-term health.

The earnings game also influences the planning and budgeting processes that businesses put in place in the name of "growth"—processes that set revenue and profit targets for growth projects without asking about the new ideas behind them and whether they will create value for identifiable customers. Strategic planning processes, which often are no more than glorified budgeting exercises, almost invariably ignore the physics of growth. Even when managers do attempt to put some real strategies behind the numbers, they often assume a one-to-one match between specific projects and financial flows. Thus, the strategy-making process pays little attention to the portfolio nature of growth investments. As one senior executive manager explained it:

> We have a portfolio view of our business. And by portfolio view I mean a PowerPoint slide. And that's exactly what it is—it's a PowerPoint slide. It does not drive our behavior. If we had ten product developments going on, we are banking on each one of those hitting at approximately the right time, generating

revenue at the right time, for us to roll up and make a plan that we are then committed to. So, it's not that we lack a strategic view of our business. I don't think we take a strategic view of our portfolio of initiatives and say that really to be successful over time I need to make sure that at least two big bets are going to come off, and over the next five years I need to have at least two products that are going to generate $50 million of revenue or $100 million of revenue annually, therefore I need in my portfolio four of those types of developments. Somehow we don't connect that kind of strategic view of the business and the markets with our portfolio of how we're actually going to achieve that.

The rallying cry becomes Supersize it! In a big organization, focus and control are key; too many new initiatives can dissipate corporate attention and resources. And so we don't want to waste time with anything small. But at what cost? The bigger-is-better mentality holds the same risks for "healthy living" in organizations as it does in a fast-food drive-thru. It actually *increases* the difficulty of finding good growth by increasing its riskiness, for obvious reasons: If it's big, why hasn't somebody already done it? And how do you tell in its infancy how big a new idea might become? Ask the folks at former PC market leader Compaq why they ignored the new business model offered by Dell and allowed themselves to lose leadership to an undergraduate starting out of his dorm room. We are betting that they will tell you that the opportunity to go direct to customers just didn't look big *enough* to risk disrupting their existing distributor relationships. Neither did offering $4 cups of coffee before Starbucks tried that small move. The impatience for big wins leads to expensive fiascos and missed opportunities.

With the obsession with size comes the notion that managers must "prove" the value of an idea before devoting any resources to it. This is, of course, a fool's errand. We state the obvious when we point out that managers asked to prove the value of a business proposition that doesn't yet exist will mostly never get out of the starting block. They would have to make up the numbers, and the only people generally allowed to do that and get away with it are expensive consultants (and until recently, investment bankers). So the best that mere managers can do is extrapolate from some data they've already got. But that kind of information is not very convincing, especially if the idea contains much that is innovative. Such information has all kinds of assumptions built into it that reflect the past and don't necessarily have anything to do with the future. It's easy to find fault with these kinds of data, and the ROI police generally do. The end result is that managers get caught in a debate about proof that never moves out of the conference room.

Making things worse, the hours spent in that conference room don't make anybody any smarter. Managers in large organizations have been encouraged to stay inside for too long, doing analysis and trying to plan the future using data from the past. While some forecasting and planning based on historical data is certainly sound—after all, that is the only data we've got to start with—relying too heavily on this approach in uncertain situations interferes with the pursuit of healthy growth. It encourages managers to abandon potentially good initiatives that don't have easily available existing data and to take more risk than is necessary (by staying with historical data rather than seeking new data from the market) in pursuing those that they do select. The kinds of processes that lead to good growth encourage employees to *leave* the building and *learn* something—from customers, collaborators, value chain partners, or even other industries.

The twin emphases on "big wins" and "proof" contribute to the disastrous prevalence of mergers and acquisitions. For decades, academic research has demonstrated that most acquisitions fail to create value for shareholders—more often, they *destroy* value—yet this cold, hard reality has done little to dampen the acquisitive appetites of organizations desperate for growth. Why? Because acquisitions seem bigger and thus more apt to be "needle movers" than organic growth initiatives, and their value seems easier to "prove" with historical data— even though this value usually fails to materialize. Paradoxically, a strong record of M&A success can actually decrease managers' appetites for the uncertainty surrounding organic growth.

Acquisitions seem more controllable and predictable—the revenue hit is certainly surer in the short term. In the long term, however, paying big premiums for ideas that a company's managers could have developed themselves seems crazy. Even more sobering, continuous acquisition in the absence of organic growth is akin to a drug addiction—it keeps taking bigger hits to get the same kick. But, in the short term, since we know that we can always fall back on the security of an acquisition when attempts at organic growth falter, there is less incentive to keep working at building a capability that seems risky and uncomfortable.

All Growth Is Not Created Equal

Some kinds of growth are healthier than others. Healthy growth is based on the *real* physics of growth, not the mythological one. It is *sustainable* because it taps into the organization's distinctive capabilities and resources to create enhanced value for customers and collaborators. This kind of growth is organic in the basic meaning of the word: related in a fundamental way to the other parts of the whole to which it belongs. Growing organically is much more than just *not* growing through mergers and acquisitions. High organic growth companies do make acquisitions, but they are generally small in size relative to the acquirer, and they serve a strategic purpose other than revenue. These acquisitions are not tacked on to the organization for a short-term high; they are fully connected to it and in service to the whole. They establish new geographic footholds or new customer segments, or they add new technology, products, services, or capabilities that can be scaled through the acquiring company's much larger customer base.

We are not talking about walking away from the organization's existing skills at execution. We don't want to throw out the baby with the bathwater. Failure to manage the existing business well will get a firm into trouble a lot faster than failing to grow some new ones. The goal is not to create "growth" organizations per se; it is to create *balanced* ones that have the capability set to excel at both invention and execution.

Most organizations today are decidedly out of balance. They look like body-builders who do only pull-ups, so they have bulging biceps (those do the heavy lifting of execution) on top of underdeveloped quads in their painfully skinny legs, which inhibit speed and adaptability—and hence growth. We need to address this imbalance while accepting that the tension between managing an organization for efficiency and control and managing it for growth and innovation never goes away altogether. Leaders don't resolve it—they work through it every day.

Where Can We Turn for Advice on Growth?

If much of what we "know" about growth is wrong, where can business leaders facing growth mandates look for good advice? Instead of turning to economics, we suggest exploring a broader selection of sciences. Physics is not the only source of good advice. Fields like biology are based on assumptions about change, evolution, adaptation, feedback loops, nonlinearity, and unexpected results. Biology has spawned new theories of change and growth that comprise an area called *complexity theory,* which asserts that growth is an *experimental learning process.* According to the theory, organizations strive for fitness, defined as the ability to perceive, adjust, and adapt continuously to an unpredictable and changing environment.[2] Scientists in this field argue that we have a lot to learn about adaptation in the face of uncertainty from the most humble of creatures: the ant. Melanie Mitchell, a professor of computer science and a member of the science board at the Santa Fe Institute, describes ants' search for food in a process she calls "communication via sampling":

> Ant foraging uses a parallel-terraced-scan strategy: many ants initially explore random directions for food. If food is discovered in any of these directions, more of the system's resources (ants) are allocated, via feedback mechanisms, to explore those directions further. . . . As in all adaptive systems, maintaining a correct balance between these two modes of exploring (random and focused) is essential. Indeed, the optimal balance shifts over time. . . . As information is obtained and acted on, exploration gradually becomes more deterministic and focused in response to what has been perceived by the system.[3]

Ants, it turns out, may have more useful advice for us than economists.

Building a "Whole Brain" Organization

Anatomy and new research on brain science are other sources of provocative insights. We've learned that the old right brain/left brain dichotomy is an oversimplification, but the fact remains that certain parts of our brain have a logical and analytical (let's just use "left brain" here as a shorthand) orientation, while others have a more expressive and creative ("right brain") orientation. Both parts of the brain have to work together, but individuals usually exhibit a preference for one orientation or the other (again, recalling the equivalent of a mental bodybuilder with big biceps and skinny legs). With the help of business education and corporate cultures, we have honed our left brains and neglected our right brains, leaving them with the equivalent of very skinny legs. Consider these differences in orientation:

analytic versus *creative*

rules versus *tools*

logic versus *emotion*

exploiting versus *exploring*

capturing value versus *creating value*

execution versus *invention*

Think of which side your organization tends to fall on. We'd bet that it is mostly on the left. Invention falls squarely on the right, so is it any wonder that most businesses are not so good at it? Like individuals, organizations need both sides of their brains working together to create healthy growth. To build a "whole brain" organization, we had better get started on those skinny legs.

Learning from Growth Leaders

So far we've turned to gamblers, venture capitalists, ants, and neuroscientists for insights into growth. We now want to add our personal observations of successful growth companies and their managers. In an effort to provide managers with concrete advice on how to face and surmount their growth challenges, a group of colleagues at the Darden Graduate School of Business at the University of Virginia studied 22 high-growth companies and more than 60 successful growth leaders in order to uncover their "secret sauce" for growth.[4] These winners helped us to identify the physics of organic growth and pointed us toward successful strategies that worked *with* rather than against them. Out of this research, we have developed what we believe to be a best practice model for achieving sustainable "good growth." Before we describe that model, however, let's look at the highlights of what we learned.

We began our studies of growth companies with several hypotheses based on our strategy backgrounds. We expected that the companies we studied would likely possess the following characteristics:

- unique products and/or services
- the best talent
- visionary leaders
- superior innovation capabilities

Counter to our expectations, none of those characteristics was necessary to produce consistently high performance. In fact, our high-growth companies

- Did not necessarily sell unique products or services
- Did not always have the best talent (but did get exceptional performance from their employees)
- Rarely had visionary, charismatic leaders
- Were not the most innovative in their industries

What these successful companies had in common were highly engaged, loyal, and productive workforces who knew their customers very well. Their leaders often were humble and passionate. These companies were master learners and imitators. They had simple, focused strategies that all employees could understand. And they seemed to have a "be better" DNA. Interestingly, in studying these high organic growth companies, we found different kinds of cultures. Some were customer-centric, some were employee-centric, some were growth-centric, some were product-centric, and some were brand-centric. It did not seem to matter. What was important was that these consistently above-average growth companies had, over time, built an enabling internal system for growth—a *Growth System*. (We'll be taking a close look at that system in Chapter 3.)

Next, we studied individual growth leaders who had beaten the odds to find growth in mature markets, despite operating in big companies that often lacked the kind of growth-enabling system described above. These managers revealed to us additional aspects of the growth puzzle and gave us our early insights about the physics of growth versus the physics of stability, predictability, and control. These growth leaders had broad repertoires of business experience that had taught them to work hard to understand the customers for whom they wanted to create value. They wanted to understand these people's lives and problems, not just sell them more stuff. This was critical to their ability to find not just new opportunities—but profitable ones that allowed them to differentiate themselves. In addition, they were consummate corporate politicians, masters at end-running the existing system (usually one based on the physics of stability), which often inhibited, rather than facilitated, their efforts. We discovered that these *catalysts*, as we called them, also had a *Growth Mindset*, along with the ability to operate the way entrepreneurs do—taking action in spite of corporate restraints, learning by doing, and minimizing risk by using only the resources they could afford to lose.

In both the company-level and manager-level research conducted at Darden, it was clear that success came from managing risk in ways appropriate to an uncertain environment: by defining clear boundaries and then freeing employees to invent and experiment. Experimentation was essential in order to learn, adapt, minimize loss, and gather data for better investment decisions.

Our final significant insight from our combined research takes us back to Silicon Valley VCs: growth, we found, results from having and managing a portfolio of initiatives. The high-growth companies and managers created a pipeline of experiments that they managed across a timeline and risk profile. The size and composition of this portfolio varied depending on the size of the business and the life cycle of its products and services. Composing and then monitoring the portfolio was one of senior leaders' primary organic growth responsibilities.

This body of research has led us to develop a model—a *Growth Formula*—that captures the essential elements involved in creating a strategic capability for healthy growth:

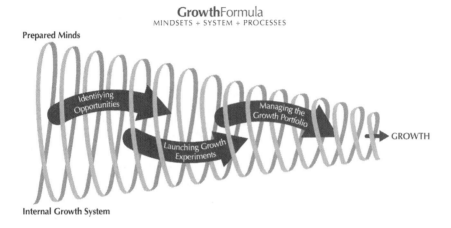

GrowthFormula
MINDSETS + SYSTEM + PROCESSES

Prepared Minds

Identifying Opportunities

Launching Growth Experiments

Managing the Growth Portfolio

GROWTH

Internal Growth System

There are three key aspects of our Growth Formula: (1) preparing employees' minds, (2) building an internal system, and (3) putting in place a path that consists of three *Growth Processes*: identifying opportunities, launching growth experiments, and managing a *Growth Portfolio*.

Who is responsible for *what* changes as specific ideas move along this path? *Senior leaders* must create and sustain the enabling infrastructure and compose and manage the portfolio of initiatives. It is the *managers'* and *employees'* jobs to be on the ground actually doing the work of identifying opportunities and moving them forward into experiments.

In the following chapters we will look at each of these activities individually, at the levels of both organizational and managerial action. Let us give you a brief preview of what the rest of the book looks like.

Chapter 2 Preview—Creating Prepared Minds

Growth depends on many human beings, with their cognitive limitations and biases, perceiving and processing information and communicating with one another along a path of exploration, invention, and experimentation amid constantly changing situations and supported by all components of the organization. Growth is an *outcome* of a set of behaviors on the part of *people*. To achieve it, individual employees need to take certain kinds of action. It is the role of the leadership of the organization to put in place an environment and a clear path that encourage those behaviors. It is also their role to ensure that the minds of employees are prepared to see and execute growth opportunities.

Scientist Louis Pasteur, explaining the role of discipline and preparation in scientific discoveries, observed that "chance favors the prepared mind." Substitute the word "opportunity" for "chance" and you've got the basic idea about the first element of our Growth System. The opportunities to grow are already there—but employees often aren't able to *see* them. Seeing them—and then leading them—requires a *prepared* mind. Creating prepared minds among employees at all levels of the organization involves attention to an individual's mindset, comfort with risk, repertoire of experiences, and "right brain" skill set for approaching the physics of uncertainty. In this world, creating prepared minds becomes much more crucial because you can't specify the rules in advance like you can in a stable world. Three components stand out as critical for this preparation.

First is mindset—a person's perspective on the world and outlook on life. Our choices reflect our mindset. For some of us, new situations are an opportunity to learn; for others, they are an opportunity to fail. Given all we've said so far about the uncertainty surrounding growth, we can't overemphasize the importance of encouraging a learning mindset in all employees. Yet many corporate cultures do the opposite—they expect perfection and punish mistakes.

Second is repertoire. Successfully leading growth can look a lot like the game "can you name that tune?" All you get is a few measures and not much time to look for the pattern. When organizations allow people to operate in functional silos, they learn to recognize and play only one song—generally "the way we've always done it." If, however, people work in a variety of functions and businesses as their careers develop, they can quickly and skillfully play a lot of different pieces of music. A broad repertoire can be an important enabler of growth.

Third is customer empathy. The word "empathy" is important here. Every company believes it cares about customers. But in many of the organizations we work with, being "customer focused" amounts to trying to shove products more effectively at people, using a variety of segmentation schemes and emotional advertising. An empathetic orientation toward customers looks quite different—it involves being deeply interested in the details of their lives as people, not categories of consumers. It is kind of a "customer inside" (to piggyback on Intel's famous "Intel inside"). This focus—and the research methods that accompany it—is much more likely to produce the kind of deep and original insights that inspire invention and lead to truly compelling and differentiated new value propositions. But detecting unarticulated needs is notoriously difficult. They don't show up in the text of market research reports based on surveys and focus groups. The successful techniques in use here are almost always ethnographic and involve close observation of what customers are trying to accomplish, not necessarily what they say they want. That is why the hearts and minds of employees throughout the organization, at every level, must be engaged in this activity.

Chapter 3 Preview—Building a Growth System

Here we will dive deep to lay out what a Growth System looks like in detail and help you assess how your current system matches up. Recall that it was this kind of internal system—not new products, new strategies, or charismatic leaders—that characterized the high organic growth companies in our research.

For our purposes, we define a Growth System as a seamless, consistent, self-reinforcing alignment of strategy, structure, culture, execution processes, leadership behaviors, HR policies, measurements, and rewards that promotes the behaviors necessary for growth—the behaviors that reflect the Growth Mindset we discuss in Chapter 2. Note that we said *behaviors,* not financial results. Financial results are outcomes that result from actions taken by people. Too often, in our experience, senior leaders jump immediately to a focus on financial results without first assessing and specifying the behaviors that can produce them.

So that's where we start—by defining the behaviors (among all employees) that promote growth as well as those that thwart it. This can be a tricky exercise for many executives, but it's a necessary first step. Asking for new behaviors in a system that still encourages, measures, and rewards the old behaviors is a complete waste of time or, worse, engenders cynicism and mistrust. For a good example of a growth-promoting and a growth-inhibiting behavior, consider the difference between saying "Yes, and" and "Yes, but." The former propels a discussion, validating and building on others' ideas. The latter is a sure conversation killer, the enemy of exploration and experimentation.

With a list of growth behaviors in hand, we then move on to building the components of the system: culture, structure, measurements and rewards, HR policies, and leadership behaviors. Often, there's not one right approach—different kinds of culture and structure, for instance, can encourage the behaviors you desire. The key is to figure out what's best for the organization. Note that changing a single element of a system to achieve new behaviors—introducing a new structure, for example, but not attempting to shift the culture or

HR policies—rarely works. The elements must be perfectly aligned and self-reinforcing to encourage the desired behaviors. And senior leaders must begin by asking hard questions about their own behaviors. To inspire you to take on this challenge, we consider some powerful examples from UPS, IBM, Stryker, Sysco, Outback Steakhouse, and Best Buy.

Chapter 4 Preview—Identifying New Ideas

Now we move to action, to the processes of growth. The first is identifying opportunities. There are almost as many myths about creativity and idea generation as there are about growth. Here we dispel those myths by showing that being "innovative" is not the purview just of artsy types; creativity works best as a team sport; some of the best new ideas aren't in fact all that new; and the first great idea we think of isn't necessarily our best.

There are two stages of idea generation: discovery and concept development. Contrary to what many businesspeople assume, innovation does not begin by considering the future. Instead, it begins in the here and now. Discovery starts with the customer's current reality and looks through his or her eyes. During this stage, we ask customers about the job they are trying to accomplish, the outcomes they want to produce, and the constraints they face. We want to pay particular attention to emotional as well as functional needs. The outcomes of this stage are the criteria a new idea must meet in order to be successful.

In the concept development stage, we finally look to the future and new possibilities, taking our customer insights and developing them into concepts that can be tested.

Where do ideas come from? To gain some useful perspective on that, we turn to the world of design. While businesspeople tend to think in terms of constraints, designers add to that possibilities and uncertainties. We can illuminate new possibilities in eight ways: *challenging, connecting, visualizing, collaborating, harmonizing, improvising, reframing,* and *playing.*

In addition to discussing the *what* and the *how* of idea generation, we also consider the *who.* Because the key here is to gather as rich a trove of ideas as possible, the search for great growth ideas must come from many sources throughout the organization. People at all levels have important roles to play: Senior leaders identify a set of strategically targeted areas of opportunity. Middle managers go after the deep insight into customers. And P&L leaders create diverse teams to carry ideas into the experimentation phase.

Involvement should be broadly inclusive. The goal is to create and maintain engaging, transparent communication and evaluation processes to gather new ideas offered from throughout the organization, acknowledge their receipt, evaluate their merit, reward participation, and clearly explain why some ideas are chosen for further exploration. Who in any organization is best positioned to see ways to improve customers' lives? Those at the front line, of course—salespeople, service employees, call center workers, and those in similar roles, who are often the most underutilized source for organic growth. Succeeding at organic growth is a volume game. Our work, as well as that of others,[5] suggests that 1,000 ideas produce perhaps 100 early experiments (we'll call these Learning Launches) that translate into about 10 initiatives in your Growth Portfolio that produce one or two "doubles" and one "home run." The more eyes on the prize, the better.

Chapter 5 Preview—Learning Launches: Doing Growth Experiments

Having accumulated, from diverse sources, an array of new business ideas, you now need to learn more about them. You begin by determining which ideas look sufficiently promising to merit moving from traditional analysis, based on existing data, into more rigorous field experiments. Managers and employees then assess each idea's likelihood, based on what they know to be true today (half-baked beliefs masquerading as truth need not apply), of passing four "tests" that determine the value of a new business offering: (1) compelling value creation for customers, (2) distinctive execution by the firm, (3) defensibility from competitors, and (4) ability to be scaled (all four of which are not created equal in the life cycle of a new idea). This requires surfacing underlying assumptions, assessing what data you've already got to test them, and then identifying what further data you could go out and get that would help you explore the critical assumptions more thoroughly.

To accomplish this (a surprisingly tricky endeavor), we have created a formal technique that we call a Learning Launch: a small, fast, low-cost experiment designed to gather data you can use to make an informed decision about the viability of a growth idea. Learning Launches involve a sequence of small moves aimed at launching and learning simultaneously. They focus on generating data and insights quickly from direct market experience, rather than on "rolling out" completed designs.

Learning Launches work because analysis has become so dominant a method for validating the worthiness of an idea and justifying the use of corporate resources to pursue it that we have lost sight of its weaknesses. There are limits to the power of analysis. Recall the physics of growth: identifying, assessing, and pursuing new growth opportunities always involves making choices under conditions of uncertainty. In most large organizations, managers pondering growth ideas are expected to take data from a known past and connect it intelligently to an unknown future. Subjecting new growth initiatives to validation through the kind of rigorous analytics that large organizations crave is a major inhibitor of growth.

Learning Launches are based on risk-minimizing behaviors that limit upfront investment—using partners instead of bringing up new manufacturing facilities, and relying on existing capabilities instead of acquiring wholly new ones. They emphasize keeping early moves simple and local—where feedback is immediate and unambiguous, where corporate politics and layers of translation don't get in the way of assessing the relationship between cause and effect.

While managers and employees are designing and conducting Learning Launches, the responsibility of senior leaders is to enable such experimentation by providing funding and decision-making processes that grant individual managers the autonomy and resources to identify and make small marketplace bets on promising growth ideas. Their role is not to screen, inspect, or attempt to manage or control individual Learning Launches early in their life. Such meddling, in our experience, slows down the process, increases fear, and generally wastes a lot of time.

Chapter 6 Preview—Creating and Managing a Growth Portfolio

In this third stage along the path, experiments will be extended and advanced as the new growth ideas that pass the four tests mentioned above are refined and commercialized by employees and gathered into a Growth Portfolio by senior leaders. This is when their window into the specific set of ideas being tested usually opens up. Their role is to compose and manage a portfolio of experiments in various states of refinement, with attention to creating a balanced portfolio of initiatives that maximize short-term and long-term opportunities while minimizing risk.

Creating a balanced Growth Portfolio involves a series of choices: Do you focus primarily on improvement initiatives—getting better, faster, or cheaper? Do you focus on innovating new products or business models? Do you undertake an aggressive acquisition strategy to fill an innovation pipeline void?

Growth initiatives vary on many dimensions. Some produce results quickly; others do so slowly. Some have an impact on the top line; others on the bottom line. They vary in the likelihood of commercial success as well as the degree of financial risk. Growth initiatives may leverage existing capabilities or require building or buying new ones. All these variables factor into creating a customized portfolio designed to maximize the probability of producing the growth needed to replace declining revenue streams from mature offerings and to maintain your competitive viability.

Here we help you categorize growth opportunities and explore some of the issues you'll encounter in managing your Growth Portfolio—whether to centralize or decentralize its management, how often to review it, and how to think about levels of investment. We also share the story of Starbucks, which developed a robust and diversified portfolio of growth initiatives—to great effect.

As we move forward, keep in mind that our intent in this book is to explore the power of aligning people, system, and processes to the real, rather than mythological, physics of growth—to make growth a *natural* act by overcoming the proclivities of organizations and individuals' cognitive make-up and left brain emphasis and instead creating more "whole brain" organizations. We'll talk in more depth in each of the ensuing chapters about what it takes to prepare managers to find and execute new opportunities, the kinds of process support they need, and the values and beliefs that underlie the system. We'll talk about how these come together to create a *strategic capability* for growth. So we are back to where we started: *people, system,* and *processes,* the enablers—and potential inhibitors—of good growth. If only we understood the physics.

2

Creating Prepared Minds

We begin our journey with a focus on the *individual*. What does it take to prepare employees for growth? In a world of uncertainty, this becomes especially crucial because you can't specify how to behave in advance, like you can in a stable world. In an unstable world, we need to rely on employees' judgment and ability, in an intelligently opportunistic way, to act in the moment.

What does an employee who is prepared to see and execute growth opportunities look like? Three components stand out as critical: mindset, repertoire, and customer empathy. Let's look at how those components play out in the story of two managers: Jeff and George,[1] two smart and seasoned managers who opt to pursue growth in markedly different ways. Jeff is an actual manager, while George is a composite based on the qualities and approaches of many managers we have worked with over the years. George helps us to bring insights from many managers into a simple comparison centered on two people. But, his characteristics should be viewed as no less realistic than Jeff's.

Two Managers, Two Different Paths

We'll start with Jeff. When our research team met Jeff, he had just joined Pfizer Consumer Products, with a strong mandate to grow the business organically. He arrived there from Doblin, an innovation strategy consulting firm, bringing with him years of experience in different businesses and functions—including the change management practice at Arthur Andersen. He had also started up two new marketing ventures.

Now meet George. George has a track record of success at his firm; he also finds himself managing new expectations around growth. His background is quite different from Jeff's, but equally impressive: an honors engineering graduate in college, George got an MBA from a top school and then joined a manufacturing firm famous for its rigorous methods and attention to execution. George has done well there and has not been interested in "jumping around" (as he describes it) to other functions or employers. He has focused on developing a depth of experience and detailed knowledge of the firm's product and its underlying technology. George is respected as the "go to" man for any technical question and has successfully run several P&Ls, profitably growing these businesses along with the market.

As Jeff was taking on his new role at Pfizer, George got an offer to take over a large but struggling business unit in his firm. He was more apprehensive than Jeff about accepting the challenge—it was clear that meeting this business's new goals would be a stretch. Having just been acquired by an aggressive global parent, the company's expectations for the growth of this division were beyond what George considered to be realistic, given market conditions. Regardless, when it was made clear to George that continued advancement with the new parent company required that he demonstrate the ability to tackle this challenge, he accepted the job.

Customers First: But How?

Jeff has acquired a strong set of beliefs in his career thus far: first, that the search for growth opportunities should begin with a deep understanding of customers' everyday lives and an ambition to make them better, and second, that innovation is a *discipline* that can, in his words, "be *learned* as a discipline— just another important dimension of what it takes to lead healthy, growing companies."

George, like Jeff, believes that improving value to customers is the surest route to increasing revenue, so he immediately asked his staff to pull together all the data the organization could find on its customers and their preferences. After weeks of study, George was confident that there was not much about the use of his firm's product by targeted customer groups that he didn't know.

Jeff, meanwhile, not content with the published market research, decided he needed more hands-on exposure to customers. He assembled a cross-functional team to "follow customers home," as he described it: to eat with them, work with them, and be involved in all aspects of their lives. Team members made thousands of observations about customers' wants and needs, and looked for emergent patterns. Throughout, they were guided by one question: "What could we be doing for consumers that would truly make their lives materially better?"

George also decided that it was time to talk with customers firsthand. Several carefully selected company salesmen escorted him to meetings with customers who seemed very satisfied. With strong relationships like these, George thought, growth opportunities should be easy to find.

Finding Opportunities: Big or Small?

Based on their deep ethnographic research, Jeff and his team identified what he called "something so fundamental it makes you want to cry." Almost every consumer health product in use, they observed, had been designed for the home medicine cabinet. As a result, consumers had to resort to various stopgap solutions for carrying health care products with them. "The insight was that we needed to provide a way for people to be able to take care of themselves and their health away from home—portable health care," Jeff explained.

He and his team then set a goal of giving consumers access to the same health care products they had at home when they traveled by car, bus, plane, or train. After a few small experiments that didn't go anywhere, they converted a bottle of Listerine—one of Pfizer's strongest brands—into a package of thin strips that fit in a pocket. They weren't sure at the outset what the potential was, but Listerine® PocketPaks®, as they called the product, seemed like an affordable bet.

George and his team were still struggling to find a "big idea." They'd been given a revenue target to hit but had no substantive strategy for getting there. Corporate had been clear that it wanted only "big wins," making a strategy like Jeff's of looking for small bets look like a non-starter. But finding those kinds of ideas wasn't proving easy. Competitors seemed to be onto the best ones already. Despite the legions of analysts (and some expensive consultants) scouring market research data, the "needle mover" remained elusive. Nothing seemed big—or sure—enough, so George and his team kept looking. To guide their search, the finance staff created some pro formas of what the financial flows of his big hit needed to look like.

Moving Ideas Into Action: Collaborate on
Small Bets or Go It Alone on Big Ones?

Meanwhile, based on some enthusiastic responses from customers to the Listerine PocketPaks, Jeff and his team quickly explored pocket-sized formats for all Pfizer brands and considered how to combine those offerings in ways that would be more convenient for consumers. Ultimately, they hit upon the idea of a portfolio of pocket-sized products that consumers could put together themselves, as they would a cosmetics kit. Soccer moms could stock kits of Neosporin ointment and Band-Aids in their cars; professionals could create kits with Motrin and Zantac for their briefcases.

George and his team also located a new value proposition they thought could be a big winner: taking a technology they had developed for use with OEM customers and adapting it for a very different group of after-market service clients. On paper, this looked like a substantial opportunity, but there were no hard data on how the new segment would react to the technology. Finance shot down George's capital budget request a few times until finally, after months spent revising ROI calculations, he got the numbers right. George's experience of being sent back again and again to "make the numbers work" is one that we often hear from managers in organizations trapped in growth gridlock. As one explained to us: "We are so data oriented and so process oriented that we do run the risk of someone comes in with a proposal and we send them back because we want them to do twenty more hours' worth of analysis to get to Six Sigma precision on this."

As George moved forward, he was also very careful to protect the firm's intellectual property: he was wary of talking too much about the new offering to potential customers or distributors and opted to self-manufacture rather than outsource. He planned a major rollout that would "take the industry by storm," as he described it to his boss.

Meanwhile, the Pfizer team was realizing that involving retailers as early as possible would be crucial. Jeff worried about getting internal buy-in—achieving the alignment necessary across Pfizer units to develop this new product-and-package combination was not going to be easy or quick. He also believed that offering theoretical arguments to retailers for the viability of this new category would not be enough. All in all, he concluded, attempting a large rollout would likely be a slow and painful process. Jeff especially believed in the need for speed:

"I think one of the things that most managers don't get—and this is the big challenge in the innovation journey—is this notion of *speed*," he notes. "An entrepreneur doesn't have the luxury of time or lots of resources. And that's why I think a lot of entrepreneurs are better at innovation than corporate executives are."

So Jeff elected to partner with a few selected retailers to conduct some quick, small-scale experiments in just a few stores. Walgreens was the first to step up to the plate, offering Pfizer limited shelf space in seven stores to test early forms of the new concept. A critical part of this experiment was observing and interviewing consumers as they experienced the product in the stores. Insights they gained from shoppers, Jeff and his team hoped, would help them test the assumptions underlying both the customer and business case for the new concept, such as how much the new, smaller sizes would cannibalize sales of the existing larger sizes.

Meanwhile, George and his team were growing increasingly worried. The news coming in from the market rollout was not reassuring. The new after-market service customer group found the product over-engineered for their purposes and didn't seem to grasp the many functional benefits brought by the new technology. Distributors seemed uninterested in adding it to their suite of offerings, and salesmen were getting discouraged. Everybody knew that George had a lot riding on this initiative; he was in no mood to hear bad news. "Failure is not an option," he repeatedly reminded his staff. "Do whatever it takes" was his response when they broached their concerns.

In Jeff's world, things were looking up. The success of the Walgreens pilots quickly persuaded competing drug stores to stock Pfizer's pocket-sized products. In the face of such demonstrated customer demand, Jeff's team was finally able to work through the territorial challenges at Pfizer, emerging with a broad array of brand new offerings. Working with retailers early in the product development process had not only cemented their interest in the new product but also convinced Pfizer senior managers, who responded to retailers' enthusiasm with increasing support for the initiative. Portable products generated 5 to 10 percent incremental revenue for the participating brands from the start and were soon projected to become a $500 million category for Pfizer (contributing to one of the highest consumer product company valuations on record when Pfizer sold the consumer products division to Johnson & Johnson a few years later).

George did not have a happy ending. After substantial losses were incurred when projected sales failed to materialize, and with little sign of a positive trajectory, the CFO pulled the plug on George's big idea. Plant assets and inventory were written off—as was George's career. In retrospect, he wondered where he, a manager with a strong track record of success, could have gone so wrong. Was it just bad luck, or was it the "black box" of innovation and growth?

We believe that it was neither bad luck nor the inherent inscrutability of the Growth Process that thwarted George's efforts: it was his (and his organization's) lack of understanding of the physics of growth. The path George chose contributed greatly to his failure. His careful application of the approaches that had helped him succeed in a stable environment actually *increased* his likelihood of failure in an unpredictable one.

Jeff, in contrast, was a perfect example of Louis Pasteur's reflections on the art of finding scientific breakthroughs: "Chance favors only the prepared mind." Jeff was not necessarily aware of this, but he had spent a lifetime preparing to find and execute growth. His experiences had helped him internalize a set of lessons for succeeding at growth: Search for unarticulated needs; expect to make mistakes; focus on placing small bets fast; and consider affordable loss, rather than ROI, as you make your early decision. Jeff's mindset, his repertoire, his understanding of his customers—and hence his tool kit—looked entirely different from George's.

The Primacy of Mindset

Success begins with Jeff's mindset—his perspective on the world and what it is all about. With his optimism and belief that, through systematic approaches, opportunities for innovation can be found and harnessed, Jeff evidences what Stanford psychologist Carol Dweck calls a "growth" mindset: the conviction that the world (including one's own abilities) can be shaped and changed.[2] For Jeff, this translates into a focus on *learning*. Because learning occurs only when we step away from the familiar, Jeff doesn't just *accept* the uncertainty that inevitably accompanies any new experience—he actively seeks it out.

For George, life is a test that he tries hard to get right so that he won't look stupid. Dweck calls this a "fixed" mindset. George lives his life trying to avoid mistakes. Because moving into uncertainty generally leads to more mistakes, George avoids that—which means that he often shies away from new experiences.

An individual's mindset is developed long before he or she enters a business organization. In Dweck's view, our early classroom experiences encourage one mindset over the other (usually the fixed wins, she argues). And the differences set in motion are profound—they establish dynamics with lifelong consequences that business organizations must pay attention to. One of these is the ability to identify and lead growth.

Dweck's mindset argument is supported by the research of other psychologists, such as Columbia University professor E. Tory Higgins. In his research on motivation,[3] Higgins notes that virtually all theories of motivation—from the time of the ancient Greek philosophers through Sigmund Freud to today—are based on the idea that we approach pleasure and avoid pain. What is less understood, he argues, are the strategies individuals use to operationalize this principle. He calls these our "regulatory focus," after the role they play in regulating our choices.

Like Dweck, Higgins sees two primary types of focus: promotion and prevention. People with a promotion focus ("promoters") are motivated by an idealized end state, which leads to a concern with advancement, growth, and accomplishment. Those with a prevention focus ("preventers") are motivated more by avoiding negative outcomes and so are concerned with protection and safety. Promoters, he argues, prefer errors of *commission*, because their inclination is to act, to pursue multiple avenues to reach their goals. Preventers prefer errors of *omission*, choosing instead *not* to act in order to minimize the possibility of a negative outcome. When promoters experience defeat, they become depressed; preventers instead become anxious. Also like Dweck, Higgins believes that early childhood interactions with caregivers shape our focus. Yet many years later, this has clear consequences for the behavior of growth leaders in business.

We believe that *organizations*, as well as individuals, take on the characteristics of either growth mindset or fixed mindset, promoter or preventer. Chances are that George works in a company that itself has a fixed mindset/preventer culture. This hearkens back to our discussion in Chapter 1 of cultures characterized by a demand for proof and an expectation that mistakes will not be made—these are classic prevention strategies. George's natural tendencies will be reinforced when he is punished for his mistakes—and sees others punished for theirs. For George, and for his colleagues, it will always feel safer *not* to try.

Jeff, on the other hand, is much less sensitive to his organization's culture and will try anyway, figuring out clever ways to work around the obstacles put in his path. He will rarely complain about how the corporation got in his way or fight internal battles; instead, he saves his energy to fight in the marketplace and then moves to a new organization when the impediments to learning and freedom of action feel too large. There's always a worthwhile new experience around the corner. And so, the organization with a fixed/preventer mindset has two serious problems when confronted with the need for healthy growth: It has discouraged its Georges and likely lost its Jeffs.

In the case of our heroes, early differences in their mindset and focus set the stage for two very different self-sustaining cycles. Jeff's tends to lead to success when the focus is on growth and innovation. George's cycle, although it has helped him succeed in a stable environment, often increases the likelihood of failure when the focus is growth.

One significant consequence of these differing mindsets is the breadth of the experiences managers accumulate across their careers. Those with a fixed mindset, like George, cling to the familiar and so tend to have a narrow range of experiences over the years. The problem is that, as we've said, learning occurs when we step away from the familiar and try something new—a fact that the Jeffs of the world seem to understand at an intuitive level. Actively seeking out new experiences—despite the attendant possibility of making mistakes—seems natural to them. They are comfortable with uncertainty—or at least understand that they must tolerate it. As a result, almost regardless of which profession they start out in, by midlife these individuals have developed a broad repertoire that spans functions and industries. University-trained engineers join R&D only to move to manufacturing and then on to a marketing role—all on the way to general management responsibilities. New accountants join CPA firms only to be lured away to a paper manufacturer or industrial products firm—or even to start their own businesses. The broad repertoires they develop are an important enabler of their ability to find growth.

Repertoire

Recall that in Chapter 1 we likened a manager's repertoire to that of a musician. When we raise managers in a functional silo, they develop deep expertise but can play only one song—and may have trouble learning new ones. Like fish who don't know that they live in water, they lack the awareness that there are many other songs, many other business models. If, however, we expose managers to a variety of functions and businesses as their careers develop, they build a large individual repertoire. In other words, they are aware of and can skillfully play many different pieces of music. This capability turns out to be highly conducive to finding new growth opportunities. New ideas don't usually come out of nowhere, "out of the blue"; they are prompted by our experiences. Opportunities lie latent, waiting to be discovered, but only some of us see them. Chances are that those of us who spot opportunities can do so because we've *already* seen them in some form or another, perhaps in a different industry. The broader a manager's repertoire, the more experiences that person has had, the more likely he or she is to see something that others with a narrower repertoire will miss.

It is important to note that a "narrow" repertoire might instead be called deep expertise; in many companies, this is an asset. But high-performing organizations, such as GE, have long believed in developing leadership talent through exposure to multiple functions and businesses. This model has a direct impact on managers' ability to see opportunities for growth. Successful growth leaders don't so much "get out of their box"—they build bigger boxes to begin with. They have "T-shaped" skills—a combination of breadth and depth. One manager we spoke with offered a case in point:

> I was a salesperson only for two years. But I kind of feel like you haven't lived until you've been thrown out of an account. The thing that was kind of interesting was you accepted that there would be some level of defeat. And the great salespeople could say, all right, that didn't work. What's Plan B? Oh, that didn't work. What's Plan C? It was never a personal thing because it was expected that you weren't going to bat 1,000. But it was also expected that sooner or later, you'd figure out how to get it done.

Repertoire should not be confused with intelligence; it is a function of experience, not IQ. Consider the difference between a skilled architect who is able to match a challenging site to a building design, not because he or she is *smarter* or more talented than a young apprentice but because the veteran has dealt with the difficulties of a site like this many times before. He or she has learned what works and what doesn't and is able to sort through a mental Rolodex of possible designs to develop a hypothesized solution quickly and efficiently. What looks like a flash of intuition is probably repertoire at work. Of course, if this sorting process mislabels the situation, this same repertoire can point the architect in the wrong direction. But the broader the repertoire, the more likely the architect is to do an accurate assessment of the nature of the problem and correctly fit a hypothesized solution to it. We find that this kind of field-based knowledge is often devalued in organizations bent on finding the highest level of B-School "talent." One manager in such an organization told us the story of his search for the right person to lead a new sales effort in an emerging market:

> We hired our first salesperson with the primary purpose really of helping us build our knowledge base. I remember some of my colleagues meeting him at the time and there was a comment that "you didn't employ the brightest light bulb" as that saying goes. And it was an interesting comment because we *deliberately* had gone out to find an industry veteran who could help teach us the industry as opposed to hiring a recently graduated fluid English speaker who

had worked for some other Western company. So he might not have been the brightest light bulb or the sharpest knife or whatever the right expression is, but he was fit for the purpose in what we were trying to do.

By the time we meet Jeff in mid-career, he has developed a broad repertoire of experiences, spanning functions and industries, that prepares him to see opportunity. By mid-career, George's repertoire is significantly narrower than Jeff's—not because he is any less intelligent, educated, or capable but because he has had less exposure to other ways of doing things.

In our studies of growth leaders, the interaction of repertoire and Growth Mindset/promoter orientation was striking. One of the memorable managers we met was hired from the outside to be president of the Mars Retail Group and charged with reinvigorating sales at Ethel M, the company's gourmet chocolates business. He had collected quite a diversity of business experience:

> When you try different businesses and do different things, you've got to learn a new industry quickly, so you need to get sharper street smarts. You start to get a feel for how business works—for how to manage people, how to spot a market opportunity, when to go faster, when to back off. I've personally benefited from being in different industries, different cultures, and different countries. It has required me to heighten my sense of feel for business.

Like Jeff, this manager believed in taking innovative ideas and quickly putting them to the test:

> When you go out with a product, oftentimes speed is as important as knowledge. So you find the balance and get the thing out in the marketplace. Then you start to understand what works and doesn't work. And if it doesn't work, it's okay. You take another shot at it. You cut your losses. You call the baby ugly.

Indeed, he also learned to see making mistakes as part of the process:

> You know what? You're going to make a bunch of mistakes. What you want to do is try and correct them. When you're younger, you don't like to make mistakes. You think that's the thing that is going to knock you off the track. You get a little bit older and get some grey in your hair, and then you realize it's okay to make mistakes. It's how you learn the most.

Repertoire does more than help growth leaders see new opportunities; it shapes how they *develop* those opportunities as well. Because these managers *expect* to make mistakes, they never put all their eggs in one basket. They adopt a portfolio-based, experimental approach, in which they conduct multiple small experiments to test their ideas. They reduce their risk whenever possible and increase their learning, as when Jeff teams with Walgreens, giving his partner skin in the game.

George, on the other hand, who is pushed to find growth despite his limited repertoire, will search ever more desperately for the one right "answer." He (and his organization) expect that ten of ten projects should succeed, and that he should be able to "prove" the value of his idea before he moves into the marketplace. Those beliefs are all fatally flawed in the context of the uncertainty surrounding growth, but they are natural inclinations of the fixed mindset.

Jeff's repertoire teaches him that there are no right answers; there are only experiments. He does not attribute failed experiments to personal failings. Instead, he recognizes that the inability to predict is a property of any new business, one of the natural laws of growth. Encouraged by both his organization and his narrow past experiences, George continues to rely on analysis in a desperate search to "prove" the value of the opportunity and to calm his own preventer-induced anxiety in the face of uncertainty. This is what he has been taught to do.

Though we all understand theoretically that it is impossible to demonstrate with historical data that a new idea, not yet attempted, will work, intelligent managers like George get caught up in this game all the time. The outcome is often gridlock. Managers spend their time recalculating Excel spreadsheets and showing PowerPoints in an effort to convince the skeptics that their numbers are solid—but of course they are nothing of the sort. And they aren't going to get any more solid without real data from the marketplace.

Worse yet, psychologists tell us that George's anxiety will make it harder for him to see disconfirming feedback from his early moves into the market, as we'll talk more about in Chapter 5. There is simply too much riding on the success of the initiative. His subordinates—and even his own brain—will tend to hide bad news from him. Deprived of accurate feedback on an idea that was not based on deep customer insight or on years of varied business experience, George is likely to fail—publicly and painfully.

Jeff, of course, fails as well—perhaps even more frequently than George—but in smaller and much less visible ways. Crushed, George will retreat to his initial view that an uncertain world is a scary place that is best kept at bay. In the future, he will avoid new experiences even more strenuously. Jeff, on the other hand, has had confirmed for him the power of trying.

Customer Empathy

The final critical component of a mind prepared to see and execute growth opportunities is customer empathy. We are talking here about much more than "customer focus." Customer empathy puts the customer's problems—rather than a company's solutions—front and center. It requires a deep interest and involvement in the details of customers' lives as people, not as categories of consumers—hence, the empathy part.

As we were casting about for a phrase to describe this kind of intimate connection with the customer, a manager we know told us a story about Cynthia—a young single mother of limited means who splurged and ordered customized M&Ms for her son's birthday party. Sadly, they arrived the day after the party. Cynthia's disappointment left an indelible mark on this manager. It wasn't merely a delayed candy delivery; it was an important moment in this family's life, and he had let her down. "I'm not customer-centric," he explained, "I'm Cynthia-centric."

Knowing Cynthia doesn't come from reading secondhand reports and market research studies. Nor does it come from the kind of "voice of the customer" work we hear so much about today; as one manager told us: "I think that 90 percent of the VOC work we do is actually wasted, because we don't really gain much by way of insight into our customers. We say 'Do you prefer the look of A versus B?' and quantitatively we're able to say that 90 percent of the customers preferred A. That's obviously useful, but it's not really giving you insight into what your customers *want to do* and what challenges they've got and how the business model is impacting them."

Really understanding Cynthia is less about her preferences and opinions and more about the ins and outs of her daily life. With that kind of knowledge, products and services exist in a context—the whole of the customer's experience—instead of the other way around. The manager's framing of the relationship with Cynthia is not "how do I sell her more of my product?" but "how can I use what I know to make her life better?" This empathetic understanding of Cynthia's life—with its human problems and challenges—is crucial for identifying truly differentiated opportunities to create value for her. It is the most important input in the search for profitable growth. If we wait for customers to *tell* us what they want, we have the same information our competitors do. If we want to get there first and stay ahead, we must make educated guesses about what they want, often before they articulate those wants.

The surest route to growth is to create better value for customers. But doing that doesn't necessarily require "out there," "out of the box" brilliance. More often, some creative recombination of ideas that are already floating around or borrowed from another industry hits the bull's-eye on an unmet (and often unarticulated) customer need.

To locate opportunities that have been there all along, managers must escape entrenched mental models and look through a different lens—"outside in," through the eyes of customers, rather than "inside out" from an organization's own needs. This results simultaneously in building deeper customer relationships and finding new avenues for growth. The number one reason growth ideas fail is that we misjudge what customers want. The surest way to reduce the risk in any project is to develop a deeper feel for that. The closer you get to customers' lives, to their problems and frustrations, the better you will be at creating value for them.

Leading-edge businesses today don't rely on focus groups and surveys; instead, they look for growth like anthropologists, observing customers in their natural setting. The search for opportunities begins when you shift your focus from "What does my company want?" to "What is the customer trying to do?" and "How can we make customers' lives better?" This invites problem-solving teams to form a strong empathetic connection with the customer, not as a data point or a demographic but as an individual with hopes and challenges worth considering. This is as true for business-to-business (B2B) sales as it is for business-to-consumer (B2C).

All products are bought by human beings, and so value can be added along both technical and human dimensions. A manager we recently spoke with illustrated for us the difference between delivering functional value to customers and situating your value proposition in the problems they experience, understanding the emotional component:

> The engineer would tell you the problem is the sensitivity of X (our product) is two percent lower. You know what the real problem is? You have nurses who are in an emergency care environment who have 20 patients in the ICU. Some of them you can't control, they're medicated, they're tied to the bed or whatever— and in between they have to use this blood gas system (our product). There's a reason why they're nurses: they don't like technology and they like people, right? But you just need to go there and look and see who the user is, what the user's daily life is, what their challenges day in and day out are to identify that they have not one second to worry about how to use the instrument.

Returning to our two managers, we can see how the existence—or lack— of customer empathy plays out. For Jeff, customers are the people he follows home—flesh and blood human beings with problems that he is trying first and foremost to understand, and then to solve. His driving question is "How do we make their lives better?" His partners and distributors are part of the answer, and he works closely with them to co-create winning solutions.

For George, customers are a set of statistics. They are targets of opportunity, and the relevant question is "What can I sell them?" When he meets them, it is in the form of a carefully choreographed royal visit from which very little learning can emerge.

George probably does know his customers' *stated* preferences—but using these as the basis for growth almost guarantees "me too" products with lackluster profitability. True competitive advantage, as we've said, lies in addressing people's *unarticulated* needs. George has no insights into those, so he cannot know what might be a truly differentiated new value proposition. He is flying blind—and pouring significant investment dollars into a single untested idea. Because he doesn't want to show his customers an "unfinished" product or risk competitors hearing about it, he ends up keeping secrets from the very people whose knowledge could help him to lower his risk.

In the end, it is Jeff who generally succeeds. George, despite all his good intentions and diligence, is a victim of his mindset, past experiences, and detached relationship with customers. Let's look at a brief summary of the dramatic differences between these two managers:

Aspects of difference	George	Jeff
Mindset	fixed/prevention	growth/promotion
Repertoire	narrow and deep	broad and T-shaped
Customer relationship	detached	empathetic
Execution approach	analyze and roll out	experiment and iterate

Is Jeff just one of the lucky few who ended up with the growth gene? He didn't need this book to learn how to prepare his mind for growth—it came naturally to him. But what about the Georges of the world, with decidedly different DNA, who can't just go out and acquire a new mindset and repertoire? Can they learn to do what Jeff does?

Based on our experience working with hundreds of managers like George, we know that the answer is yes. Jeff is not resorting to magic to achieve growth; he is using a set of tools routinely practiced by successful innovation firms—tools that we will discuss in the remainder of this book. When he follows customers home and explores their lives—not just their use of his product—Jeff is using ethnographic techniques that companies like Xerox have been using for decades to study how people interact with office equipment. There is nothing new here.

When Jeff doctors up quick and dirty physical examples of the pocket-sized health products, he is using a prototyping technique long practiced within R&D. And when he enlists Walgreens as a partner in his small experiments, he is practicing customer co-creation, long recognized by innovators in many industries as the surest way to de-risk a new offering.

Finally, when he makes small bets fast, he is simply generating and testing hypotheses about his new business concept—this is the scientific method, which most of us learned in the fourth grade: he surfaces the key assumptions and looks for data to test them. Today's business culture has pushed them to be so analytically oriented that the experimental method does not come easily. We have forgotten that the best data in an uncertain environment come from real-world trials, not extrapolations of the past. So a tool like assumption testing, that structures the process, is essential to help wary "fixed mindset" folks like George feel safe trying something new.

This is just another aspect of leadership development, and a few key tasks stand out:

1. *Help George understand how his deeply embedded ways of thinking and behaving impede his success as a growth leader.* To build this awareness with executives, we use the DiSC® Leadership Profile, a psychological assessment that has been taken by more than 40 million over the past 50 years. Designed to assess people's preferences for how they work within their environment and respond to uncertainty, the instrument divides behavior into four dimensions: Dominance (D), Influence (I), Steadfastness (S), and Conscientiousness (C). Individuals who are a high D tend to have a bias for action; they have a Growth Mindset/promoter focus and so are comfortable moving forward in the face of uncertainty, even if doing so will result in errors. Those errors, as we discussed earlier, will be errors of commission. A high C individual, on the other hand, needs considerably more data in order to feel comfortable enough to act. This is the fixed mindset/preventer focus at work. This person prefers errors of omission and believes that no action is better than action that risks failure.

These differences often lead to tension between managers driving growth (who tend to be high Ds) and those whose support they need (who may be high Cs). Recognizing that the roots of this tension are differing levels of comfort with ambiguity, rather than being inherently "good" or "bad," can help George manage both his expectations and his team more effectively.

High C managers (like George) can start by identifying personal preferences that may have contributed to their past success (for instance, a certain perfectionism is important in engineering) but are actively impeding them as growth leaders. There's some good news for George: Managers with engineering backgrounds, we have found, are often the most enthusiastic about learning the processes and tools associated with growth and about applying them with discipline back on the job—once they come to understand and accept the physics of growth.

2. *Broaden George's repertoire by exposing him to other businesses and to people with different perspectives.* It's clear how to do this with people early in their careers—through, for example, the rotational assignments common in high-performing organizations. But what about a mid-career manager like George? For someone at his stage, rotations are expensive and deliver a much lower payoff. We need other ways to address the deficiencies in the repertoires of mature managers.

The answer is teams. The narrower a manager's repertoire, the more critical his or her growth team becomes. Part of George's problem may be that the rookies and outcasts were assigned to his team. Rather than compensating for George's weaknesses, these people exacerbate them. The rookies themselves have no repertoire to call on—they were planning to rely on George's. The outcasts—well, they were probably the people sitting around with time on their hands, while the high-performing managers were too busy (and important) running the existing business to be pulled off that and put on George's team. And if someone stepped in to train the team, it was probably the wrong kind of training.

Case in point: an e-mail arrived not long ago from the head of Learning and Development at one of the organizations for whom we design executive learning experiences. It read:

> We want to invest in helping our managers to grow their businesses in these tough times. However, we are being very fiscally conservative—the investment must be proven. Our Corporate Business Development function is shifting to build a cadre of professionals who can apply quantitative rigor to investments being made by the business. Can you help us?

How familiar does this sound? We are in recovery from the greatest financial meltdown in our personal histories; anxiety is widespread, not just about the economy but about life in general. Leaders are wrestling with an unprecedented level of uncertainty. Like most organizations these days, this one is responding in the way that seems sensible—battening down the hatches, cutting costs, and stepping up the rigor of the review process for new ideas. Investment capital is scarce, so the bar must be set higher to get any of it. Levels of scrutiny multiply. Nobody wants to put a dollar at risk that they don't have to.

This well-meaning strategy has pernicious effects, for all the reasons we've been discussing. Answering that query was not difficult: We suggested that he didn't really need us, that it would be most effective and efficient—and humane—to shoot himself and the rest of the Business Development staff in the foot immediately and without our help. Despite the best intentions, this organization is setting itself—and its managers—up to fail. Everything we have learned about how managers succeed at growth and innovation points in the opposite direction from the path that the organization behind this e-mail has chosen.

But back to assembling a growth team. It's critical to start by enumerating the capabilities and qualities you need. Experience and broad repertoires must be at the very top of the list. The idea that growth and innovation projects are good training for newly minted MBAs is dangerous. Such experiences may provide useful learning for the young recruit, but they are unlikely to provide successful growth outcomes for the organization. Our research is clear on this point: You maximize your chances for success at a growth project when you assemble a multifunctional and diverse team of experienced hands. Commercial experience—including significant face time with customers—is especially important. As one of the successful leaders we studied told us:

> We're not going to take a risk on execution. We'll give it to somebody who knows how to start something. We are not testing that particular person—they have already proven their ability. All we're really testing is what's the market activity for this?

Another echoed those thoughts:

> You've got to safeguard people and give them that opportunity to take on difficult cases, because otherwise you will not get there. You want your most talented people solving your most difficult challenges. And you want to make sure that they feel that they are supported and if they fail it's okay, it's part of their development process. And the most challenging problems are not necessarily ones that have the highest revenue or size. It's hard to find people who can do that.

3. *Help George surface the assumptions behind his mindset and behavior.* One of the clients who first asked us to help develop growth leadership capabilities

in their staff was in the nuclear services business. As trained nuclear engineers, their fixed mindset/prevention focus was, understandably, extreme. Even some of our own colleagues were skeptical that individuals with such deeply seated values around accuracy and safety could be persuaded to take even calculated risks. These engineers quickly taught us otherwise. They were perfectly capable of adjusting their risk barometer when the downside was a lost sale rather than a destroyed community. But nobody had ever suggested that they should adopt a different tolerance—or why. When they understood the unintended consequences of unilateral thinking about risk and acquired a few new tools for managing it, they were off and running.

Both Dweck and Higgins believe that mindsets and regulatory focus can be changed; we are all capable of seeing the world both ways. But not without awareness and attention. George needs reminding of times when he has tried new approaches and succeeded. Mindset and regulatory focus are also sensitive to environmental influences—a topic that we will turn to in Chapter 3 when we look at Growth Systems and the importance of corporate culture.

4. *Get George out of his office and interacting with customers to learn how his product or service solves—or fails to solve—their problems.* Here, we are not talking about staged royal visits. George needs exposure to unhappy customers as well as satisfied ones. The former have a lot to teach him. A successful growth leader explained to us:

> I tell my sales team, "Don't ever take me to a customer that is going to say something good about what we're doing. I love to hear that, but don't take me there. What are they going to tell you: 'You're doing a good job, thank you!' That's a five-minute phone call. Take me to somebody who would never buy from us or who is extremely unhappy with us. That's where learning comes in."

George needs to follow that advice.

5. *Inspire George by sharing stories of managers like him who have mastered an alternative approach to achieve growth.* People need compelling stories to show them what the future can look like—but not stories of Steve Jobs and the kids at Google! They need stories about managers who look like them and operate in mature businesses and bureaucracies, where finding growth is challenging and executing on it even more so.

6. *Give George time to focus on growth.* Growth leadership is not a job that can be done after normal working hours or in snatched moments here and there. It takes time and sustained attention to develop a deep knowledge of customers and to design and conduct experiments. If a manager is forced to

choose between putting out a fire today and investing time in the future, the future will lose 99 percent of the time. No matter how many Covey seminars we attend, the urgent almost always wins over the important. Organizations serious about achieving organic growth need to face this fact: Growth and innovation are inherently messy and seemingly inefficient, and they require slack to accomplish. That is a hard pill to swallow in today's "do more with less" environment.

This approach to growth may look expensive, but think of what George's failed "big idea" cost his organization in management effort and dedicated resources—not to mention the dampening effects of that failure on the enthusiasm for risk taking in the culture writ large.

7. *Teach George a new set of tools.* These are the tools we talked about earlier—tools borrowed from the innovation world. They include customer journey mapping, prototyping, and assumption testing. When George's mind is prepared for growth, we are ready to get him started using these tools as he begins the process of identifying opportunities for growth—the topic we turn to in Chapter 4.

It is obvious that the ultimate way to help George adopt a new mindset would be to surround him with a supportive organizational system and culture. Such a system would make it safer for him to "fail" (and help him reframe failure as learning). It would reward him for trying. And it would give him processes and tools to structure his efforts.

In Chapter 3, we talk about preparing an organization for growth by aligning culture, structure, HR processes, measurement and reward systems, and leadership behavior to encourage engaged employees to behave in new ways consistent with succeeding in the environment of uncertainty that surrounds growth.

3

Building a Growth System

We focused in Chapter 2 on the individual. Now, we are going to turn our focus to how the organizational environment either promotes Growth Mindsets and behaviors or inhibits them.

Growth is not a predictable linear process but an iterative learning process requiring the right mindsets, organizational environment, and processes. As we discussed in previous chapters, the mindsets, organizational environment, and processes that enable growth are different from the mindsets, internal environment, and processes that facilitate exploitative execution. That is the challenge—to manage those tensions or differences so that the result is both excellent growth exploration and exploitative execution.

Consistent business growth is more likely if leadership (1) creates an organizational environment that promotes growth behaviors and deters behaviors that inhibit growth and (2) behaves in ways consistent with that environment. That enabling organizational environment is what we call an internal Growth System ("System"). Systems enable both individual and organizational Growth Mindsets, growth behaviors, and the utilization of the Growth Processes that we will discuss in Chapters 4, 5, and 6.

What Is a System?

A system is a combination, ordering, or assemblage of things or processes that work together to produce a more complex result. A system can be an alignment like our solar system. It can be a combination of organs, blood vessels, and muscle like our digestive system. Systems are common in engineering, biology, complexity theory, and the cyber-intelligence field. In a system, the different components interact with one another to create more than the sum of the parts.

For our purpose, a Growth System is a seamless, consistent, self-reinforcing alignment of culture, structure, leadership behavior, HR policies and processes, and measurements and rewards that enable and promote defined growth behaviors:

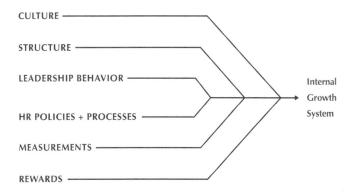

Note that we are talking about behaviors, not financial results. Behaviors produce financial results. For each desired growth behavior, each part of the System has to be designed to send consistent positive messages.

The Discovery of Growth Systems

This concept of a Growth System came from research of companies that produced consistent, above-average growth for more than five years. Such companies are rare. At least six academic studies[1] have found that less than 10 percent of the companies studied produced above-average growth consistently for more than four years, and less than 5 percent did so for more than seven years. A study of over 20 of those companies in greater detail to find explanations for their sustained growth produced surprising findings. Contrary to common management theories, these consistent growth companies did not have differentiating strategies or the best talent or visionary leaders or even unique products or services or the lowest-cost products.[2]

What these companies did have were Systems that produced a highly engaged workforce, humble passionate leaders, and a learning environment of constant improvement. Creating and maintaining a Growth System is hard work—so hard, in fact, that a System can become a differentiating competitive advantage. Maintaining a System requires near maniacal sensitivity to actions, policies, and communications to ensure consistency. This is crucial because inconsistencies or mixed messages from any part can dilute a System's effectiveness. These Systems are very sensitive to inconsistencies because inconsistencies create hypocrisy and destroy trust.

Where have we found such Systems? Best Buy, Costco, UPS, Southwest Airlines, Starbucks, Tiffany & Company, Room & Board, Levy Restaurants, Stryker, McDonald's, TSYS, Ritz-Carlton, Outback Steakhouse, Walgreens, Whole Foods, IBM, and Sysco are some examples of companies that have created Systems.

Defining Growth Behaviors

You probably are asking, "How do we create a Growth System when we already have an existing culture, structure, HR policies, and measurement and rewards policies? Where do we start?" You start by defining the beliefs and behaviors that enable growth in the context of your strategy and capabilities. The purpose of the Growth System is to promote certain behaviors, so before you build the system you must define those behaviors.

There is no single growth behavior that will transform a business into a consistent high-growth company. Growth beliefs and behaviors include:

• Actively listening to others	• Asking questions	• Trying new ways
• Seeking out different views	• Having a positive attitude	• Collaborating
• Being curious	• Challenging existing ways	• Constructive debate
• Sharing information	• Being emotionally engaged in your job	• Supporting experimentation
• Learning from mistakes	• Acting humbly	• Trusting your manager and leaders
• Not placing blame	• Treating people with respect and dignity	• Contributing to an energizing positive work environment
• Teaching, not punishing	• Measuring and rewarding people fairly	• Removing obstacles to growth
• Encouraging diversity of opinion	• Finding meaning in your work	• Being paranoid about complacency

If you want consistent growth, then you must embed in your business critical inquiry, constructive debate, collaboration, diversity of views, listening, trying new ideas, tolerance for mistakes and failures, and learning. And you must enable, measure, and reward behaviors that create that result. As importantly, leaders and managers must personally model the desired behaviors and remove obstacles to those behaviors for others. One of the leaders who built such a System described it this way: "You celebrate success, console failure, and get rid of people who are afraid to try new things."[3]

If you want growth, you want the opposite of "group think," "command and control," "keep your head down," "we know everything," and fear environments.

In working with leaders in designing Systems, we have seen that it is very difficult in the beginning of this defining process for many to think at a granular level about behaviors. It is much easier to think about strategy and to define financial results. We have found one technique helpful in facilitating this defining of growth behaviors. Start with defining the behaviors that inhibit or limit growth. The desired behaviors obviously are the opposite of those bad behaviors.

The following four questions have been helpful in facilitating the process of defining growth behaviors:

- What behaviors encourage or evidence a Growth Mindset?
- What behaviors evidence a fixed mindset?
- What behaviors promote or evidence utilization of growth-creating processes: identifying opportunities, experimenting, and building Growth Portfolios?
- What behaviors inhibit the effective utilization of growth-creating processes?

Here is an example of such a list we created for one of our consulting clients:

Good Growth Behaviors	Bad Growth Behaviors
• Active open-minded listening	• Being closed minded and not listening
• Asking "why" and being curious	• Accepting the status-quo/rarely questioning
• Engaging in critical inquiry	• Avoiding critical inquiry
• Challenging underlying assumptions	• Rarely examining underlying assumptions
• Embracing new experiences	• Avoiding new experiences and learning
• Participating in critical debate	• Avoiding debates
• Thinking about ways to improve	• Waiting to be told to improve
• Exploring customer needs	• Thinking you know what customers need

Continued

Good Growth Behaviors (cont'd)	Bad Growth Behaviors (cont'd)
• Looking for ways to improve	• Waiting to be told what to do
• Being comfortable with uncertainty	• Disliking uncertainty
• Acting humbly	• Acting arrogantly
• Having an action bias	• Having a procrastination bias
• Participating in experiments	• Avoiding experiments
• Participating in idea generation	• Infrequently participating in idea generation
• Sharing knowledge	• Hoarding knowledge
• Seeking different opinions	• Being comfortable doing it my way
• Treating mistakes as learning opportunities	• Hiding mistakes or fearing mistakes
• Having a proactive mindset	• Having a reactive mindset
• Forming cross-functional teams	• Avoiding collaboration
• Encouraging different opinions	• Stifling different opinions
• Engendering trust	• Acting inconsistently
• Having difficult conversations	• Avoiding difficult conversations

After you define the growth behaviors you want to encourage, then you are ready to align your System to promote and enable the good behaviors and to inhibit and penalize the bad behaviors. The starting place is culture.

Culture

In starting with culture, we are not talking about the formal culture statement a company may have published on its website or in its annual report. We are talking about the beliefs and unwritten rules of how companies actually behave—not what they say, but what they do. We have never read a company culture statement that said, "The only thing we care about is financial results; our employees are fungible commodities used to produce those results; and our customers are our dumb sheep to be shorn." Yet, some companies act that way and treat both their employees and customers that way.

Cultures vary, and there is no single formula for a Growth System culture. Some companies, like Sysco and Best Buy, have cultures based on customer-centricity.[4] Others, like Tiffany, have a culture based on protecting and enhancing the brand.[5] Room & Board built a culture of meaningful relationships with its suppliers, employees, and customers.[6] Others, like Southwest Airlines, Outback Steakhouse, TSYS, Starbucks, and Levy Restaurants, have employee-centric cultures.[7] Others have product-centric cultures.

It is important to note that none of the consistent high-growth companies studied had a culture based solely on creating shareholder value. While all believed in creating shareholder value, all focused, at a minimum, on one other stakeholder: customers, employees, and/or society. These companies had a multiple stakeholder model. When you get inside these companies, the daily mantra is not "Grow, grow, grow to make quarterly earnings," the mantra is "Be better, better, better so we can better serve our stakeholders." The common theme across all of these companies is constant improvement. Growth was not the major message. Being better to serve stakeholders was.

Constant Improvement

Our thinking has evolved as we have researched, taught, and consulted with more companies to the point that we think that constant improvement is likely the core building block that can create a company-wide learning and growth exploration mindset. Why? Because constant improvement requires consistently challenging the way you currently do things (no matter how successful you are), engaging in constructive dialogue, encouraging diversity of opinion, engaging employees in daily doing their job better, faster, and cheaper, routinely trying new approaches, and having a willingness to change. Constant improvement requires learning and experimentation. Constant improvement can become the foundation from which growth exploration can occur.

Think back to the tension we described in Chapter 1 between exploration and execution. Almost all of the consistent high-growth companies we studied excelled at both. Constant improvement was the common bridge between the growth explorers in the company and the employees who were focused on execution exploitation—growth farmers.

For constant improvement to occur, you need a paranoid view of success and complacency. You also need to encourage critical inquiry, constructive debate, and realistic assessments and collaborations, have an action bias, view mistakes and failures as learning opportunities, communicate clear guidelines where and under what conditions people can try new things, and encourage employees and customers to be engaged in creating and experimenting with new growth ideas.

Experimentation and learning are less likely to occur in cultures of conformity, cultures of fear, cultures of "go along–get along," cultures of "my way or the highway," cultures of "that is how we have done it for years," "top-down command and control" cultures, and in cultures that devalue employees and/or customers.

One final point that cannot be overemphasized: The behaviors of leaders and managers either reinforce or destroy the environment needed for sustained growth. If you want consistent growth, we advise that you start with an examination of yourself: Do you really have a Growth Mindset and behave in a manner that enables growth behaviors in your employees and colleagues? If not, how and when are you going to change?

An example of a constant improvement culture that enables both execution excellence and growth exploration can be found at UPS.

The UPS Culture[8]

UPS was founded in 1907 by 19-year-old Jim Casey, who borrowed $100 to start a home delivery service for Seattle department stores. Today UPS has revenue of over $50 billion, 400,000 employees, and operates in more than 200 countries. UPS has been a consistent high-performance company for years. UPS is operationally a large airline and a large trucking company with one of the world's largest data processing and radio network centers. It delivers over 15 million packages a day to over 8 million customers 99 percent defect-free and on time. In the United States, its largest package processing facility (Worldport) comprises over five million square feet (90 football fields) with a perimeter of over seven miles. UPS is big.

UPS's 85,000 drivers hold esteemed positions. The average tenure of a driver is over 16 years, and driver turnover is less than 2 percent a year. Union drivers can earn up to $70,000 a year, and senior drivers receive nine weeks of paid leave a year and 100 percent of their health insurance is company paid. More than 25 percent of the company's U.S. managers are members of minority groups, and women represent around 27 percent of its U.S. management team. Historically, more than 70 percent of its full-time managers were promoted from within. UPS employee turnover is less than 6 percent annually. Even though UPS's labor costs are higher than those of its main competitor—because UPS's workforce is 46 percent unionized and its full-time workers are employees entitled to benefits and not independent contractors—year-in and year-out UPS is a market leader. How can this occur?

To understand UPS you have to understand its culture and how that culture brings together the key beliefs that drive employee and leadership behavior. UPS's culture is based on its founding values of integrity, quality, dignity, respect, stewardship, partnership, equality, and humility. These values are operationalized by an integrated three-prong culture:

1. A performance culture in which everyone is accountable to everyone else, regardless of position
2. A "constant challenge, be critical, be better" culture known as "constructive dissatisfaction"
3. An employee-centric ownership culture in which executives are stewards of the business

Mutual accountability means that every employee is accountable to every other employee. Accountability means doing what is right and doing it well. This mutual accountability applies to every employee, including the CEO, who symbolizes his accountability to all employees by having a special phone in his office on which any employee can call him directly at any time to talk about any issue.

UPS employees are viewed as partners, and this mutual accountability leads to a more egalitarian culture that devalues status, position, and elitist perks. All UPS top management have offices of the same size, share administrative support, and eat in the company cafeteria. These executives drive themselves to work and fly on commercial airlines, following the same travel policies as employees. Self-marketing is frowned upon. At UPS, it is not about you—it is about the team.

Constructive dissatisfaction leads to relentless improvement. The words *constructive* and *relentless* at UPS are purposeful and descriptive. This "be better" culture goes back to 1921, when Jim Casey began building an internal industrial engineering capability to focus on internal productivity and efficiency. Over the years UPS espoused the view that "in God we trust, everything else we measure." This measurement mentality promotes an environment of never being satisfied with the way things are because they can be improved. Dissent, inquiry, questioning, and challenging current ways are valued and encouraged because they are the behaviors that make UPS better.

UPS is also an employee-centric company in which leaders are stewards. Jim Casey believed that good leaders built up others and took a sincere interest in the welfare of the people they worked with, making all employees feel like they are the company. Employee-centricity is made real through promotion-from-within policies, employee stock ownership plans (it is commonly stated that UPS has more millionaire truck drivers than all other transportation companies combined), diversity programs, employee education programs, and internal free agency programs that give employees opportunities to grow and advance.

The UPS System is designed to engage every employee emotionally in being part of the UPS way, which is being better today than we were yesterday and sharing in a meaningful way in the results through better pay, benefits, career advancement, and ownership in the company. UPS's three-prong culture is mutually reinforcing, sending a consistent message: We are all in this together, and we will all do well if we all do our part, and if we do, we all will be treated fairly. This message is intended to encourage growth-producing behaviors and discourage complacency, arrogance, hubris, and fixed beliefs.

UPS's three-prong culture fits together nicely and consistently to drive the behaviors that are important to UPS. UPS understands that culture, leadership behavior, measurements, rewards, and HR policies have to consistently work together to create the environment and to reinforce desired behaviors. Creating this fit is part art and part science. Success comes when you get all the parts working together in a seamless manner to send consistent reinforcing messages. Success is fleeting unless you are paranoid about systemic inconsistency and hypocrisy.

Thinking about UPS's behavioral objectives may help you think about yours. What are UPS's objectives? Are they to create a team in which people hold one another mutually accountable for execution excellence—being better every day—while treating one another as equals with respect and dignity? Are they to provide team members with opportunities to grow and share in the financial results of their work through promotions and ownership? What are your behavioral objectives? We hope they are more than meeting next quarter's earnings target. While we focused here on culture, the point needs to be emphasized that UPS created a System—a UPS recipe that combines the right ingredients (culture, leadership behavior, measurements, rewards, and HR policies and processes) in the right amounts to produce a consistent high-performance growth organization.

IBM's Turnaround

Another example of the importance of culture is IBM's turnaround under Lou Gerstner, which began in 1993 upon his joining IBM. During the preceding two years, IBM lost over $16 billion—yes, $16 billion—and downsized 40,000 employees. IBM had a history of being a very successful company, but its success led to complacency, rigidity, and fixed mindsets unwilling to consider anything that differed from the IBM way. IBM had a consensus-driven culture that was lethargic and immune to change. Gerstner arrived and saw that IBM's problem was itself, and he quickly introduced a new culture at IBM that was both customer-centric and employee-centric—not IBM-centric. Gerstner turned around IBM in two years, but what is interesting for us is what he learned in the process: "I came to see, in my time at IBM, that culture isn't just one aspect of the game—it is the game."[9]

To change IBM, Gerstner not only had to change its culture, but to get the desired behaviors he had to change its organizational structure, its measurements, and how it compensated people, including executives. Gerstner had to get all the parts aligned to enable and motivate the new behaviors IBM needed in order to rebound. After changing IBM's culture, Gerstner made changes to the other components of IBM's System to send consistent messages that enabled, promoted, and rewarded the new desired IBM behaviors.

As Gerstner learned, cultures encourage and reward—or discourage and punish—certain behaviors. You have to get culture right in order to create your System. A culture of constant improvement that promotes diversity of opinion, critical debate, and dissent can mitigate complacency and group arrogance, and result in an exploratory, curious, "try it" environment.

Culture Lessons

What do UPS and IBM have in common? UPS created and has maintained a culture that has propelled its growth and consistent performance for years. Gerstner at IBM had to create a completely new culture to return IBM to a position of industry leadership that continues today. While the circumstances differ in those two stories, what is consistent is that it was necessary to create an internal System that aligned culture, structure, leadership behavior, HR policies and processes, and measurements and rewards to drive the desired behaviors.

Let's move on to structure. What have we learned about structure as a growth and innovation enabler?

Structure to Grow

Structure comes into play in two ways in creating a Growth System. First, an organizational structure has to promote and enable the positive behaviors we discussed above. Second, structure has to promote the utilization of growth development and testing processes (we will discuss those in Chapters 4, 5, and 6) that can create new ways of doing business and new customer offerings.

Structure is the answer to the questions of how and what you decentralize to give more autonomy and permission to encourage people to explore and do growth experiments. Structure is the result of managing the tensions between centralization and decentralization and between entrepreneurial experimentation and low-variance execution. Structure either facilitates change, experimentation, and innovation or makes it so cumbersome and bureaucratic that it stifles it. We know that growth results when managers are allowed to act more like entrepreneurs than bureaucrats; and we know that successful growth companies act more like a "small company soul" in a big company body.

There is no single structure that fits every business. The best structural design will depend on the industry, the business model, and the capabilities of the organization. There are three common structural approaches to facilitating growth: (1) ingraining innovative exploration inside execution businesses; (2) segregating exploration in separate research centers that serve operating business units; and (3) a hybrid model where exploration activities are separated from the business units during their development and commercialization stages and then are either spun off into new business units or spun back into existing business units.

Exploration Inside

The first common structural approach to growth is to ingrain growth exploration inside exploitative execution businesses. This is what we find at Best Buy, UPS, and Sysco, which expect their business units to be great at both execution and growth. To implement its new Customer Centricity business model, Best Buy[10] made every store a separate business unit. This structure enabled the necessary behaviors of store management and employees to execute the business model of customer-centricity and solutions selling. This structure made each store manager an entrepreneur with responsibility and autonomy to manage that store's activities to drive desired ROA numbers, while taking into account its customer demographics and needs. This entrepreneurial "act like an owner of your store" mentality puts the responsibility for generating local-market ideas at the level closest to the customer. It also gives local managers and employees the freedom to experiment and try new ideas.

Sysco[11] operates its business through more than 140 business units. It frequently splits a business unit into two units when it "folds out" part of a business to free it to be more entrepreneurial. Sysco gives all its business units substantial leeway (autonomy) in areas it calls the "front of the house," which are customer-facing, but gives business units little if any freedom regarding "back of the house" areas: accounting, capital, food quality, brand reputation, and legal. Sysco wants to promote entrepreneurial fast action to meet customer needs and to remedy customer issues. To do this, operating units have lots of rope. The company's former president calls this "NIHBIDITA:" "Not Invented Here But I Did It Anyway."

Another company that used structure to drive entrepreneurial behavior is Stryker Corporation,[12] a medical device and equipment company. In its high-growth phase, Stryker experienced over 20 consecutive years of more than 20 percent annual compounded growth. This growth was enabled by the adoption of a holding company structure that made each business unit a separate entrepreneurial company with its own decentralized support functions. As Stryker grew and these business units prospered, Stryker would split a successful business unit into two smaller units to re-energize entrepreneurial behaviors and to create more leadership positions and employee growth opportunities. Stryker placed responsibility for growth inside each business unit, closest to the employees charged with understanding and meeting customer needs daily.

Levy Restaurants,[13] the leading player in food catering for sports and entertainment arenas, similarly makes each sports venue a separate business unit and gives entrepreneurial freedom to the chefs and managers to meet the needs of that location's customers. Like Sysco, Levy Restaurants keeps control of quality and food sourcing at the corporate level. Again, like Best Buy, Sysco, and Stryker, Levy believes that people closest to the customer will know better how to improve and innovate quickly to meet customer needs. As its CEO stated, "I constantly remind our leaders that very few customers ever walk into our corporate offices."[14]

Exploration Outside

The second common structural approach to promoting growth exploration is to segregate it in a separate research center that serves operating business units. This is common in the pharmaceutical, biotech, and engineering or science-based industries. Corning and United Technologies are two examples. This structure allows them to use dedicated staff, processes, and investment dollars to do exploration. In these companies, developing new offerings can take years of experimentation and requires dedicated protected resources. For these companies, growth happens best when it is segregated from core operating execution businesses.

Exploration Greenhouses

IBM illustrates the third model. As part of the Gerstner transformation to generate growth faster, IBM created a separate unit called Emerging Business Opportunities (EBOs), responsible for the development and commercialization of new growth initiatives. EBOs were intended to free entrepreneurial exploration from dominating execution mindsets and processes and to dedicate resources to exploration. After going through the iterative development process and commercialization experiments with customers, if the EBO growth initiative proved viable it would be adopted by an existing business unit for further development and scaling, or the EBO could become a new business unit. Separating growth experiments is seen in some companies as being necessary to prevent the dominant execution mindsets, processes, and low tolerances for variance in the operating business from stifling or killing growth experimentation and exploration. Unlike the example of research centers, these EBOs can become separate operating business units.

Some companies use a process similar to the EBO process, keeping some growth exploration in existing business units while removing some growth initiatives from the business unit. This approach to the structure question has evolved over the past two years in one of our consulting clients. This company has four separate business units. Each business unit ranks growth ideas by risk and the degree of unknowns into one of three groups. Growth ideas ranked low-risk with few unknowns are owned by a business unit product team, which has the autonomy to experiment. Growth ideas deemed to be medium-risk with more unknowns require business unit approval for experimentation. Cross-functional diverse teams are created to do the experiments, with those teams reporting to a business unit committee. Lastly, if a growth experiment involves high risks and many unknowns or is outside the boundaries of existing capabilities but is deemed worthy of exploration, it is transferred to the corporate growth group for exploration management, drawing upon corporate resources across business units. Broadly, the more novel a growth idea, the more protection, patience, and development it needs. In some companies, especially those with an unhealthy obsession with making quarterly earnings, growth exploration has to be removed from business unit management's responsibility.

Removing Structural Impediments to Growth

Structure sometimes can inhibit growth experimentation when multi-layered approvals are required to do a growth experiment, when operating units are not allocated capital for experimentation, and when business units do not have the autonomy to create multi-functional teams to do an experiment. To address potential structural impediments to growth, rather than ask "What is the *best* structure to enable more growth experimentation," some companies have asked, "How does our structure inhibit growth?" with the objective of removing those growth inhibitors.

Most companies operate structures with several different business units supported or controlled in varying degrees by a central headquarters group.

Many times these business units become impermeable silos that inhibit cross-business-unit knowledge sharing, collaboration, and teaming. As companies move from product-centricity to customer-centric solution selling to differentiate themselves from the competitors and ward off product commoditization, silo busting becomes necessary. Often matrix structures are created to encourage the desired behaviors. Unfortunately, shifting to a matrix structure alone generally does not produce the desired behavioral change. It is also necessary to align culture, leadership behaviors, and measurements and rewards to drive collaboration, teaming, and knowledge sharing.

Business structure is important macro-organizationally because it can either facilitate or inhibit growth exploration behaviors. Structure is important micro-organizationally in determining where and under what protective structure your businesses can conduct the growth experiments that will be discussed in Chapter 5. The purpose of creating a protective structure, whether inside or outside a business unit, is to remove growth experiments from the dominance of execution mindsets and low tolerances for failure, placing growth experimentation in a protective and nurturing learning environment.

Measurements and Rewards

The next critical step in fostering growth in a business is to align measurements and rewards to promote the desired growth-producing behaviors. There are two fundamental rules of management. First, if you want certain results, measure those results. Second, if you want those results done well, then measure and reward those results. Measurements and rewards, just like all parts of the System, are interconnected. In this part, the focus will be on measurements. Rewards will be discussed in the Human Resources section that follows.

Measuring Behaviors

As we said earlier, thinking about growth resulting from granular behaviors is not how many executives think about growth. Nor is figuring out how to measure those behaviors. Before continuing, it may be helpful to look back at the lists of good and bad growth behaviors earlier in this chapter.

Some of those behaviors can be measured by numbers: number of growth ideas generated, financial impact of improvements, number of experiments conducted, time spent with customers exploring needs, populating knowledge management content, utilization of knowledge management content, proficiency in Growth Processes (Black Belts), and speed, for example. Other behaviors, however, are harder to measure numerically but can be assessed through 360-degree evaluations.

Every manager in a growth company should be evaluated 360 degrees on his or her Growth Mindset and whether he or she encourages or discourages critical inquiry, the exploration of new ideas, constructive debate, voicing of different opinions, and "trying" something new or different, and whether he or she punishes growth failures, engages employees in growth ideation processes, seeks employees' input, and is arrogant or domineering, for example.

It is important to stress that designing measurements is not a onetime event. Sysco, for example, has been engaged in measuring employee and manager growth behaviors for over 20 years. Its CEO said to us a few years ago, "We still are working at getting it right."[15] Creating growth behavioral measurements is an iterative process, just like the other Growth Processes we discuss in this book. The key is to start. The following is an example.

"Yes, and" or "Yes, but!"

We are constantly amazed at the power of the phrase "Yes, and" compared to the phrase "Yes, but." "Yes, but" shuts down discussions by rejecting without examination and exploration what is being offered. "Yes, and" keeps a conversation going and can lead to critical inquiry and learning and maybe even a growth experiment. Company teams have experimented with measuring the use of the phrase "Yes, but" within teams and its effects compared to the phrase "Yes, and." While these experiments did not rise to the level of scientific experiments, consistently reported results from over 450 managers are that increasing the use of "Yes, and" and decreasing the use of "Yes, but" had significant impact. Teams had better discussions that resulted in more critical inquiry and debate, and more employees were willing to voluntarily and proactively participate in the processes.

Behaviors lead to outcomes, so the measures you design must reflect the outcomes you are seeking. If you want more growth ideas, then measure ideation. If you want more experimentation, then measure frequency of experiments. If you want more constant improvement, then measure it at the employee level.

In working with companies to put in place measurements of desired growth behaviors, we have learned that 360-degree reviews are necessary to measure many of the desired behaviors. They can be a good starting point from which to iterate numerical measurements.

So far, we have explored the System components of culture, structure, and measurements. Now, let's move to human resource policies and processes.

Human Resource Policies and Processes

Human resource policies, processes, and programs ("HR") are integral to creating a seamless, consistent, self-reinforcing System. HR has to enable, hire for, train for, design, and implement measurements, as discussed above, and reward the desired behaviors. Aligning hiring, training, and evaluation processes with growth behaviors is critical but often overlooked. These HR practices, if thoughtfully designed, can influence how fully employees emotionally engage with their work and their overall level of satisfaction.

In our study of consistent high-growth companies, we found that high employee engagement and satisfaction were a common denominator of these companies. As a senior leader at Best Buy stated, their most important financial measurement is employee satisfaction because moving that measurement up even one-tenth of a percent has significant positive financial impact.[16]

Why are high employee engagement and satisfaction so important in companies like UPS, Sysco, Levy Restaurants, and Best Buy? If daily execution excellence and daily constant improvement are the foundation of exploitation and exploration, those activities must occur throughout the organization. Who must perform those activities? All employees must. So is it likely that employees who feel like they are respected, listened to, treated fairly, and given opportunities to personally grow will perform those tasks better than employees who feel the opposite? This seems to be the case. Emotionally engaged and satisfied employees seem to take execution and improvement to a consistently higher level. High employee engagement and satisfaction also lead to lower turnover and higher productivity, both of which impact net profits positively.

High employee engagement in these companies was enhanced by promotion-from-within policies; stability of HR policies; perceived fairness of compensation, review, and promotion actions; frequent constructive feedback; egalitarian (except for pay) team cultures; devaluation of manager and leader elitism; stock ownership; and humble steward leaders.

Stability of HR compensation and promotion policies is important. If you are asking employees to constantly learn, change, and improve, then keeping the "rules of the game" (as to how people are rewarded for playing the game) stable and consistent builds trust in your System. One company that has proven the value of high employee engagement is Sysco.

Sysco

Sysco[17] has been the market-leading wholesale food distribution company in the United States for years. It delivers over four million cases of food daily to over 390,000 customers 99 percent on time and defect-free. It employs over 45,000 employees, over 50 percent of whom are hourly warehouse and delivery personnel. Its market share and profit margins are significantly higher than those of its competition, yet it basically sells commodity products. How does it consistently achieve such stellar results?

It's the Sysco System that enables, promotes, and rewards execution excellence and entrepreneurial behavior at the customer-facing positions: truck drivers, salespeople, and restaurant business review consultants.

Sysco's measurements show the financial impact of high employee engagement. The following chart compares certain measurements across two different groups. The first group includes all the employees working in Sysco business units that achieved top quartile employee satisfaction as compared to all Sysco business units. The second group includes all employees working in business units that achieved bottom quartile employee satisfaction as compared to all Sysco business units:

Business Units Work Climate Impact

	Work Climate Average	Operating Pretax %	Operating Expense as a % of Sales	Workers' Comp. % of Sales	MA Retention	Delivery Retention	Associates per 100K Cases
Top 25% work climate	4.01	7.5	13.3	.07	85	88	4.13
Bottom 25% work climate	3.61	5.3	14.9	.20	72	78	4.33
Variance	.40	2.2	1.6	.13	13	10	.20

These numbers demonstrate the difference in employee performance in high employee engagement (top 25%) and low employee engagement business units (bottom 25%). Top quartile employee satisfaction business units earn significantly higher operating pretax profits, have lower operating expenses, and achieve higher employee retention and productivity. These are meaningful differences and show that at Sysco high employee engagement has positive financial implications.

What are the HR policies that contribute to those results? Sysco thinks that they are having over 65 percent of employees owning stock in the company and the promotion of people from within to fill open positions 95 percent of the time. Many of Sysco's hourly workers are paid weekly incentive bonuses, which rewards them frequently and close in time to good behaviors. The power of rewarding good behavior was expressed by Rick Schnieders, the former chairman and CEO of Sysco, this way:

> [Our] culture was self-replicating. Our people feel good because many own stock, and they see results when everyone works hard and performs. Many, including our truck drivers, are on incentive bonus programs and see compensation results directly and weekly. All of this makes people work harder—they feel good about the results in which they share, and they feel good about working hard tomorrow, etc.[18]

Another market leader that created a System that resulted in high employee engagement is the Outback Steakhouse chain.

Outback Steakhouse, Inc.

Outback has an employee-centric culture that is "tough on results, but kind on people." It has a philosophy of teaching, not punishing, and "no rules—just right," which gives employees leeway to make things right for customers. Outback's goal is "to be a company of goodness—to our guests, to our employees, and to our communities."[19] Outback's System is designed to drive entrepreneurial behavior and ownership at the local level. Hiring and training are local responsibilities. Much like Sysco, Outback gives restaurants significant autonomy for customer-facing activities while centralizing and standardizing food quality and food preparation activities.

At each Outback restaurant, the manager and the chef own an equity share of the restaurant, and the rest of the employees participate in bonus programs driven by the restaurant's performance. Outback thinks it has created more restaurant manager millionaires than any other restaurant chain in the U.S. When we visited them, one of the founders of Outback told us, "We believe that when you get to the top, you have to remember to send the elevator down to bring other people up." You will recall UPS's belief that it has more millionaire truck drivers than any other distribution or transportation company in the U.S. Ownership of a share of your results, directly or indirectly, is important to many employees.

In the study of consistent high-growth companies, ownership played an important role in driving high employee engagement. Ownership means more than actual stock ownership. Not every company studied had broad employee stock ownership. But what they did have were HR policies and behaviors that gave employees some control over their destiny. "I feel like if I take care of the company, it will take care of me," was the kind of sentiment their employees expressed. They believed that if they performed well, the company would treat them fairly. They trusted the System.

Other Examples

Other companies that have created high-employee-engagement environments and have achieved consistent high performance are: Southwest Airlines, Starbucks, AFLAC, Chick-fil-A, TSYS, Whole Foods, Wegmans, Ritz-Carlton Hotels, Levy Restaurants, SAS, Zappos, Patagonia, and Yum! Brands. While high employee engagement does not guarantee high performance, it appears that they occur together frequently.

Leadership Behavior

All of the work done to create a seamless, linked, aligned, self-reinforcing System (culture, structure, HR policies and processes, measurements, and rewards) that enables, promotes, and drives defined growth behaviors will be for naught unless leadership (from the CEO down to managerial levels) models the desired behaviors. As in the Best Buy example discussed earlier, leadership must "walk the talk."

Leaders must not only model the desired behaviors but also eliminate their own bad behaviors. Leadership behavior inconsistent with the desired behaviors has negative impacts far greater than just the impact in the particular interaction. That bad behavior creates hypocrisy, which destroys trust, and the bad behavior is deemed to be okay by others and will cascade down an organization.

The CEOs of the consistent high-growth companies we have studied were humble, passionate operators who believed in stewardship and serving their stakeholders. They managed themselves and understood the major impact their behavior could have on the organization. They understood the profound role that their daily behaviors had in either reinforcing or destroying the environment needed for growth. They believed and behaved as if employees were far more important than themselves. They fought executive elitism and devalued executive perks other than compensation. Even with respect to compensation, you rarely see any of them in the lists of highest-paid CEOs.

In many cases, the biggest growth inhibitors in a company are leaders and managers who are not able to model the desired growth behaviors. Unfortunately, in some cases creating the holistic type of System we are talking about requires a major firing or retirement in order to send the message that certain behaviors will not be tolerated.

It's the System

As we conclude our exploration of the power of an internal, seamless, consistent, self-reinforcing, aligned System of strategy, culture, structure, HR policies and processes, measurements and rewards, and leadership behavior to drive desired growth behaviors, we need to emphasize a few points.

Building a System takes hard work and time. Maintaining one requires constant vigilance and a heightened sensitivity to inconsistency among any of the components and in messages. These Systems are fragile in that bad behaviors, hypocrisy, or inconsistency in any of the parts can have a large negative impact. Successful Systems (evidenced by consistent high performance) can also be challenged by major changes in leadership. This is particularly true if a new CEO comes in from another company and makes major people and cultural changes.

System building requires senior executives to focus part of their time on working *on* the company, not solely *for* the company. Think of your System as your unique recipe made up of your "secret" ingredients in the right amounts to generate your unique growth environment. A well-designed and maintained System can become a compelling differentiator that leads not only to consistent high performance but also to a competitive advantage.

Let's look at a successful company that changed its business model in an attempt to gain even more strategic advantage over its competitors. In order to change its business model, Best Buy had to change its System—every component had to be changed and aligned to drive the new desired behaviors. Best Buy, like UPS and Sysco, is a good example of an aligned Growth System that drives defined growth behaviors.

Best Buy's New System[20]

In 2004, Best Buy was the market leader in consumer retail electronics, operating more than 800 big box retail stores in the United States. Best Buy realized that it needed to further differentiate its customer value proposition from its competition and adopted a new business model called Customer Centricity. Customer Centricity meant that Best Buy would not sell products but would consult with customers and help customers meet their needs by creating solutions for them. However, traditional retail push product sales techniques and traditional retail measurements would not work if employees were to behave more like consultants. What did Best Buy have to do to implement its business model?

First, it defined the behaviors that its employees needed to exhibit to implement the new business model. It then had to create a System that enabled and reinforced those behaviors. Best Buy wanted its store salespeople to listen to customers, to ask questions in order to understand customer needs, to classify customers according to their needs, and to suggest combinations of products and services to meet specific customer needs. These behaviors were very different from the existing behaviors of pushing products, especially those products in the distribution center.

To enable and promote these new desired behaviors, Best Buy had to change its culture, its structure, its leadership model, and its measurements and rewards. Best Buy had to turn its command-and-control, top-down culture and structure into an inverted pyramid so that customers became "kings and queens," employees became "royalty," and managers and leaders became servant leaders. With this cultural change came a structural change: each store became a separate operating business unit, giving operational ownership to store management. With this change in structure came new store measurement and compensation policies that were put in place to drive entrepreneurial store-level behaviors.

Not only did employee behaviors have to change but mid-level and senior management behavior had to change, too. To promote humble, serving-others behavior at the senior level, Best Buy made 20 percent of senior management bonus and stock option compensation dependent upon "walking the talk" as a servant leader. Best Buy's vice chairman stated:

> Our mission as leaders is to put in place something that will live on—be sustainable. It is a constant battle of paradoxes: entrepreneurial versus bureaucracy; fighting complacency and self-satisfaction, which result from success; and to keep rejuvenating the core business and to look for new geographies or concepts for the future. Managers have to live our values—20 percent of their annual option grant is dependent upon whether they walk the talk. If you want to work at Best Buy, leave your ego at the doorstep.[21]

Conclusion: Assessing Your System

In our teaching and consulting, we use a tool that we developed called the Growth System Assessment to illuminate the presence of growth inhibitors, non-alignment, and bad growth behaviors. On the following pages is a mini-assessment for you to use to start your thinking about how you can create your own System to enable and promote a Growth Mindset and behaviors. This tool should help you think about the steps you need to take to improve your organizational growth environment:

Growth System Assessment ©

Which statement best describes your organization or yourself? OR Which statement is more true or correct?		
1. Culture		
Our culture encourages debate and dissent	v.	Our culture encourages conformity and "go along–get along"
Our culture encourages experimentation	v.	Our culture discourages deviating from established ways
Our culture accepts mistakes as a necessary part of learning	v.	Our culture punishes mistakes
Our culture rewards diversity of opinion	v.	Our culture rewards conformity
Our culture encourages teamwork across business units	v.	Our culture does not encourage cross–business unit collaboration
Our culture encourages broad knowledge sharing	v.	Our culture encourages knowledge sharing on a need-to-know basis
Our culture results in a "one way" mentality	v.	Our culture encourages challenging current practices
Our culture is product-centric	v.	Our culture is customer-centric
Our culture most values its people	v.	Our culture most values financial results
Our company is risk averse	v.	Our company encourages taking measured risks
We are paranoid about any mistakes	v.	We accept that mistakes are a given when trying new things
Before trying new things, we have to study them and prepare a business plan	v.	We have a fast way of doing small experiments
Our company is driven primarily by quarterly earnings	v.	Our company is driven primarily by a long-term view
We are a proactive company	v.	We are a reactive company
We value speed and action	v.	We value deliberation and caution
We value learning	v.	We value not making mistakes
2. Structure		
Our structure enables speedy flexible responses to customer needs	v.	Our structure inhibits speedy flexible responses to customer needs
Our structure gives authority to customer-facing employees	v.	Our structure gives little authority to customer-facing employees
Our structure transfers new ideas from the field to senior management quickly	v.	Our structure does not quickly transfer new ideas from the field to senior management
Our structure enables quick decisions	v.	Our structure inhibits quick decisions
Our structure requires many levels of approvals on small matters	v.	Our structure gives managers authority to make many types of decisions

Which statement best describes your organization or yourself? OR Which statement is more true or correct?		
3. Leadership Behavior		
My manager encourages different opinions	v.	My manager discourages opinions different than his or hers
My manager frequently seeks my input on changes	v.	My manager just informs me of changes
My manager punishes all mistakes	v.	My manager understands that mistakes will occur in trying new things
My manager rewards compliance and "going along"	v.	My manager rewards constructive inquiry
My manager likes to learn	v.	My manager only cares about meeting his performance goals
4. Employee Engagement		
Most people I work with feel that the measurement and reward system is differentiating and fair	v.	Most people believe the measurement and reward system is political and does not fairly differentiate
You can advance here and be all you can be	v.	Advancement is limited to those who play the game the best and who do not make waves
My manager seeks my feedback on how he performs as a manager	v.	My manager rarely seeks my feedback on those issues
5. Measurements		
I am measured on learning and constant improvement	v.	I am not measured on whether I constantly improve
I am asked to give 360° reviews of my managers	v.	I am not asked to do such reviews
I am measured as to whether I create cost savings or productivity ideas	v.	I am not so measured
I am measured as to whether I create new revenue ideas	v.	I am not so measured
6. Ideation Processes		
I am encouraged to submit ideas for growth and improvement	v.	It is not important that I submit ideas for growth or improvement
People who submit ideas for improvement are thanked	v.	People are only acknowledged if their idea is deemed a good one
7. Experimentation Processes		
We have a company process to test out new innovation or growth ideas	v.	We do not have such a process
Everyone is expected to think innovatively	v	Innovation is the responsibility of a special group
I have received training on innovative thinking	v.	I have not received such training
I have received training on opportunity recognition	v.	I have not received training on opportunity recognition

I have received training on how to do a small cheap test on a new idea	v.	I have not received such training
I am encouraged to spend some of my work time on thinking about new revenue growth initiatives	v.	I am not encouraged to do so
New ideas must go through a business plan process with financial return hurdles	v.	New ideas can be tested without a formal business plan
Managers have the authority to run experiments and test new ideas	v.	Such experiments must be approved by senior management
Managers have authority to conduct experiments and test new ideas	v.	That is the responsibility of a separate group
8. Alignment		
Our culture, leadership model, what we measure, and what we reward are aligned and consistent	v.	We do not consistently measure and reward desired cultural and leadership behaviors
We teach, measure, and reward growth-producing behaviors, not just financial results	v.	We primarily measure and reward financial and productivity results
Most employees own stock in the company	v.	Most employees do not own stock in the company
We primarily promote from within	v.	Many times we hire from the outside

4

Identifying New Ideas

In the previous two chapters, we have laid out the foundational elements of our Growth Formula: prepared minds and an internal Growth System. Together, these form an organizational environmental that enables growth. Now it is time to move into action, to chart the path of growth itself. This path comprises three processes: identifying new ideas, transforming promising ideas into experiments, and composing and managing the portfolio of experiments an organization needs to achieve its growth goals. In this chapter, we examine the first process: idea generation.

As managers, we pride ourselves on our expertise at evaluating and executing on ideas. We have developed a wealth of tools, techniques, and metrics to guide us, from return on investment (ROI) analysis to PERT charts. *Generating* ideas, however, is another matter. Idea generation seems like voodoo. In this strange land, we fear, all is magic: you either have the creative chops to conjure, or you don't. And most managers are pretty sure that they don't.

Here again, as we said in Chapter 2, our research on successful growth leaders tells a different story:

- A deep understanding of customers' unarticulated needs provides a sure route to growth.

- A manager's repertoire of experiences sets the stage for the kind of opportunities he or she is able to see.

- Finding good ideas is a volume game. The trick is to generate multiple options, learn how to evaluate them quickly, and then invest or move on.
- Mistakes come with the territory. Expect to make some.

In this chapter, we will focus on a systematic approach to idea generation that involves two stages: brainstorming and concept development. We will also examine four sources that converge to contribute to finding a great idea: senior managers (who set strategic themes), frontline managers (who bring local knowledge to identify specific opportunities), internal capabilities (which determine what our distinctive skills allow us to do), and customers (who tell us what is worth doing).

Let's be clear here about the *kind* of new ideas that we want to generate. What makes ideas great is not hard to figure out. There are three components: customers want them, we are the right firm to make them happen, and we can do so profitably. In Chapter 5, we will talk in more depth about each of these characteristics and how we test for them. Our emphasis here is on locating them.

Myths About Creativity

The origin of great creative ideas has been the source of almost as many myths as there are about growth: myths about who can be creative and how, and even about what creativity is. Let's take a few minutes to dispel them so that we can get to the truth about idea generation.

Myth 1: Only certain kinds of people can think creatively.

Our research challenges common beliefs about what "innovative" people look and act like, where we find them, and how they do what they do. Meet Dave Jarrett of Crowe Horwath, one of the largest CPA firms in the United States.[1] Dave joined the firm in 1975 and spent the next 20 years there as an auditor and tax expert. He was then asked to head up an internal group tasked with generating ideas that would deliver better value to Crowe Horwath clients in profitable ways, while enhancing the firm's capability set.

Dave's challenge was a daunting one—for many reasons. Perhaps the most obvious was that few people saw accounting and tax firms as hotbeds of creativity. Dave knew that he and his colleagues were generally stereotyped as linear thinkers, not well-suited to seeing and developing creative new ideas. They were also seen as risk avoiders—reluctant to try unproved things out of fear of damaging important client relationships.

Yet Dave knew that innovation required a willingness to take some risks and pursue "out of the box" solutions. He and his colleagues would need to learn to accept failures in the process, but failure, he knew, was expensive: a working prototype often required an investment of more than $25,000 in new software. Dave also believed that clients ought to be involved much earlier in discussions about the value of new ideas—but again, his colleagues were reluctant to show their clients "unfinished" work.

Dave wondered whether there were ways to surmount these obstacles, so he started looking for new approaches and tools. He found these in use at innovation and design firms like IDEO and applied them to the innovation process at Crowe Horwath. He brought together multi-disciplinary teams and used all the knowledge in the room to brainstorm new solutions and then translated these quickly into simple, low-cost prototypes. These prototypes often took the form of simple storyboards, which he and his colleagues used to engage clients in a conversation about the potential of the new idea to meet their needs. On the basis of clients' feedback, Dave and his group would iterate toward what they hoped was a better solution and then seek additional feedback as to whether they were on track.

The storyboard sessions, Dave emphasized, were never about trying to *sell* clients something. They were about understanding the extent to which the new idea created value for clients and soliciting information on how to improve it.

From a financial viewpoint, Dave's approach was much less expensive than prior practices. Furthermore, Dave's colleagues discovered that clients enjoyed the conversations. As Dave explains it: "So now we've got a few hours invested in the storyboards and some guys going out and meeting with their clients. Even if the idea goes nowhere, there is always value in meeting with your client. Plus the client feels valued because you cared to ask them what they thought. So there is never a downside to that. And we have saved ourselves a fortune."[2]

Dave is just one of the people we've met from many walks of life—some of them accountants, engineers, and nurses, as well as managers—who have demonstrated that our beliefs about who is and is not "innovative" are just plain wrong. These people can bring as much innovative spirit to an organization as those in marketing and R&D, provided they are given the right tools. Creative thinking is not a "black box."

Myth 2: Creative people need to work on their own, like the lone genius in his atelier.

Because it is so dependent on experience, generating new ideas works much better as a team sport, involving a diverse group of people who share a purpose and have deep customer insight. Numerous studies, in fields as distant as conflict resolution and new-product development, have demonstrated the power of cognitive diversity within a group to improve decision quality. Frame-breaking questions, so essential to the kind of generative thinking we are looking for, often come from those with different perspectives. The most successful growth teams are cross-functional and so include the perspectives of all stakeholders—customers, value chain partners, manufacturing, marketing, R&D, and finance, to name just a few.

But generating ideas requires learning together and communicating well—not always easy across a diverse group. The development of a shared sense of purpose and vocabulary is key. People must be willing to engage in both trying to understand the perspectives of others and self-analysis. The focus is both on making one's own assumptions and strategic logic available to the group and on seeking to understand the assumptions and logic of others. This sets the foundation for uncovering the kind of superior solutions that tap the group's perspectives and competencies. The challenge exists in maintaining a balance between creating a team culture that shares a vocabulary and sense of purpose, and continuing to welcome dissent and divergent views.

The ability to have a high-quality conversation is a function of the skill set and the mindset of those involved. We've talked at length about the importance of a learning mindset—about the importance of seeing oneself on a journey of learning—but managers also need to develop a learning skill set. This involves mastering two very different ways of communicating, which Peter Senge calls inquiry and advocacy:

> Most managers are trained to be advocates. . . . Individuals often become successful in part because of their abilities to debate forcefully and thus influence others. Meanwhile, inquiry skills go unrecognized and unrewarded.[3]

Inquiry skills are especially crucial during the discovery phase of the idea generation process. Listening to customers in order to understand them rather than to sell them something presents the same kind of inquiry challenge as listening to a colleague with divergent views. And this can be an entirely new experience for managers, who are often programmed to sell and to advocate. We find that specific attention to this new behavioral skill set is essential for their ability to contribute to a group involved in creative work.

Myth 3: Creativity is about novelty.

This may well be the most pernicious myth of all—the idea that an idea must be wholly new to deserve the label "innovative." The kind of ideas we want to generate—the kind we'll call creative—are all about *creating new value for customers.* We don't care if it's already been tried or looks like "old wine in new bottles" or has been borrowed from another industry. Does it create value for your customers that no one else has yet offered them? If the answer is yes, congratulations! You've got a winner. Chances are, *most* of the components of the valuable ideas generated will have been floating around in some form or another—perhaps for decades.

In his review of significant innovations spanning hundreds of years, Steven Johnson argues that what we are really looking for is "a collection of building block ideas, spare parts that can be reassembled into useful new configurations."[4] Even fundamentally disruptive innovations like the printing press, the light bulb, and the Internet were recombinations of existing parts—"more bricolage than breakthrough"—he argues.[5]

Myth 4: We know a great idea when we see it.

Wouldn't that be nice! Unfortunately, as we've already said, it is very difficult to determine the potential of a nascent idea. Sometimes it takes only minor tweaks to unlock significant value: think about bottling water or putting wheels on luggage! This is one of the reasons why we need lots of small experiments to give us lots of options.

This idea of embracing multiple options turns out to be surprisingly challenging for managers. Though it seems obvious in theory, in practice it can feel wasteful—why worry about chasing lots of ideas when you only need one really good one? But often, the really, really good one is not the first idea we come up with—more likely it's the fourth or fifth. Or maybe it turns out not to be nearly as good as we thought. If we yield to the temptation to stop after we get the first good one, we may miss out on the extraordinary one and find ourselves with all our eggs in the wrong basket.

This is a well-known problem in creative fields like architecture and photography. Members of the faculty committee at Case Western Reserve University tell a wonderful story about working with the internationally renowned architect Frank Gehry to design a new business school building.[6] There were serious concerns about whether the needs of the faculty, students, and administration could be met within the available square footage. The Gehry team labored long and hard to create a design that could meet all those needs. After this design had been shown triumphantly to the faculty committee, committee members watched in horror as the architects tore it up! This was just to show it could be done, the architects advised them; now they could get on with creating even better designs! In fact, when asked about the greatest challenges he faced as an architect, Gehry cited the tendency of clients to fall in love with the first design. Getting them to keep the design "liquid" enough to explore multiple options was extremely difficult—but essential to breakthrough designs. Similarly, National Geographic photographer DeWitt Jones always reminded himself that a great shot didn't mean he was done for the day. It just meant that he'd had his first best shot.

Here's the good news about these myths: there are tools and techniques to help us debunk them, but they are not the ones we generally teach in business school. They are, instead, the kind that have been practiced for decades in innovation firms like IDEO. There are tools for both phases of the idea generation process: discovery and brainstorming and concept development. It is beyond the scope of this short primer to explore them here, so we've included a list of some of the key tools to get you started:

Design Tools

For Discovery

There are three important discovery tools that we believe will be of significant value to managers seeking growth: *journey mapping, value chain analysis,* and *mind mapping.*

Journey mapping is a tool for developing a deep understanding of customers' experience as they seek to get a job done. It assesses the existing experience through the customer's eyes, noting the steps a customer has to take when using the existing technology or service. It pays particular attention to the emotional highs and lows accompanying these steps. These are the blind spots that are often overlooked.

Value chain analysis reviews the current value chain that supports the customer's journey. How does a solution engage value chain partners to deliver the value that a customer will pay real money for? It assesses the capability set that a firm brings and looks for strategic opportunities and vulnerabilities in their value chain footprint.

Mind mapping generates insights from exploration activities and uses them to create a set of criteria that a new idea must meet in order to be successful, in terms of both customer value and corporate profitability. It provides the output that drives the second stage of the idea generation process: concept development.

For Idea Generation

This stage includes *brainstorming* and *concept development* tools.

Brainstorming generates new possibilities and business models. It avoids working in a vacuum by bouncing ideas off a small group of trusted friends and coworkers—letting insights generate more insights.

Concept development assembles innovative elements into a coherent alternative solution that can be explored and evaluated. How does the puzzle fit together? Can you take it apart and put it together differently in a way that will add more value?

Source: From *Designing for Growth* by Jeanne Liedtka and Tim Ogilvie. Copyright 2011 Jeanne Liedtka and Tim Ogilvie. Reprinted with permission of Columbia University Press.

The Two Stages of Idea Generation
Stage 1: Discovery

Since the goal of innovation is to envision and implement a new future, it is always tempting to start the search for new ideas there. Many businesspeople believe that innovation starts with brainstorming. But it actually starts in the here and now. This is where the search is most likely to be fruitful, in a place that scientist Stuart Kauffman called "the adjacent possible."[7] Johnson describes it as "a shadow future hovering on the edges of the present state of things, a map of all the ways in which the present can reinvent itself."[8]

This is often difficult for busy, hard-pressed managers to accept. First, it seems as though starting our search for the future in the present will doom us to incremental change. Not so, if we ask the right questions (more on this shortly). Second, businesspeople tend to want to jump to answers very early in the process of looking for new ideas. Unfortunately, those top-of-mind solutions are often based on preconceived notions about what customers want or what competitors are doing. Innovative ideas that provide the best opportunity for differentiation and superior profitability come from deep insights about customers' current reality. Without those insights, the imagination has little to work with.

The quality of the discovery process determines, to a significant degree, the quality of your growth ideas—this is where growth initiatives are won or lost. This first stage sets the foundation for success.

Discovery starts with the customer's current reality aTnd looks through his or her eyes. Despite our avowed passion for being "customer focused," in many situations this comes down to trying to shove existing products more effectively at customers using a variety of segmentation schemes and emotional advertising. For the managers we studied who were succeeding at growth, it means something quite different—being deeply interested in the details of customers' lives as people, not categories. Remember the story in Chapter 2 about the manager who told us that he had abandoned being "customer-centric" in favor of being "Cynthia-centric"? That is what we are talking about. So it is time to stop advocating and start practicing those inquiry skills we talked about.

The reason why talking to customers so often seems like an innovation dead end is because we ask them the *wrong* question: "What do you want?" Human beings, sadly, are notorious for being unable to envision something they haven't seen yet, so not surprisingly, their answers usually take the form of "me too" products and incremental enhancements (and that is after they give up on asking for lower prices). This is why Tom Peters called the customer "a rearview mirror."[9]

During discovery we are going to ask our Cynthia a set of questions focused on the *job* she is trying to get done, the *outcomes* she wants to produce (including the metrics she uses to measure them), and the constraints she faces. Understanding her ultimate aim and what is getting in the way is the best way to uncover needs with high value potential—but ones that she often can't articulate when asked directly. We are going to pay particular attention to her emotional as well as functional needs. Attending to Cynthia's emotions in the B2C space may seem logical (we know she wants to feel like a good mom when she buys those customized M&Ms) but less useful in the B2B space. This is an illusion. Your business buyers, assuming that they are not robots, have emotional needs as well. They want to look good in the eyes of their boss, and they may feel insecure and in need of reassurance. We believe that understanding the customer's journey can offer even greater advantage in the B2B space because this approach is still uncommon and its power untapped.

The outputs of the discovery process are the criteria that a new idea must meet in order to be successful. It's important to capture these criteria in a formal way so that what has been learned is carried into the next stage. We suggest that you use the following template:

Design Criteria

Design Goal
- What have you learned about the target customer?
- What needs (functional, emotional, psychological, social) does the design have to fulfill for the target customer?
- Why is it strategically important for your organization to address those needs?

User Perceptions
- How important is your proposed offering to the target customer's well-being?
- Are there aesthetic attributes necessary to succeed with the target customer?
- Does the target customer expect the offering to have certain social, ethical, or ecological attributes?
- What does ease-of-use mean to the target customer?

Physical Attributes
- Must the offering be able to capture, store, and /or transmit information about usage?
- Does the offering need to be designed for use in specific environments or situations?
- Are there weight or size considerations for lifting, use, or transport?
- Are there memory, bandwidth, or connectivity issues?

Functional Attributes
- Does the design of the offering need to accommodate specific use-case scenarios? List them in order of importance to the target customer.
- Does the design need to address compatibility or standards issues?

Constraints
- Does the final offering need to be completed by a specific date?
- What constraints does your current business impose (the offering must use the existing manufacturing base, provide higher profit margins than current offerings, leverage proprietary technologies, etc.)?
- Are there ecosystem and regulatory concerns (height of shelves at retailers, OSHA regulations, etc.)?

Source: From *Designing for Growth* by Jeanne Liedtka and Tim Ogilvie. Copyright 2011 Jeanne Liedtka and Tim Ogilvie. Reprinted with permission of Columbia University Press.

Stage 2: Brainstorming and Concept Development

Finally, we get to the new ideas part! Having thoroughly explored and documented the current situation, we can now look toward the future and new possibilities. This is when we need to take a creative leap, and most businesspeople dread it. This stage includes brainstorming and then a distinct concept development activity. Managers hate brainstorming, we know, but this time it is going to be different. You've got great customer insights, translated into design criteria, to help you. The key is to approach brainstorming the right way and couple it with concept development to translate ideas into concrete, fully developed concepts. Concept development assembles innovative elements into a coherent alternative solution that can be explored and evaluated.

Again, generating options is important. We capture the output of this stage in a series of "napkin pitches":

Napkin Pitch: [concept name]

Need	**Approach**
• What customer wants this? • What unmet need(s) does it serve?	• What asset or capability does this leverage? • How would it create value? • How will our company create a sustainable advantage?
Benefit	**Competition**
• How will the customer benefit? • How will our company benefit? • What other parties will benefit?	• What firms currently serve this need? • How will they respond to our entry?

Source: From *Designing for Growth* by Jeanne Liedtka and Tim Ogilvie. Copyright 2011 Jeanne Liedtka and Tim Ogilvie. Reprinted with permission of Columbia University Press.

Where Do New Ideas Come From?

Now that we are moving into actual idea generation, we need to face squarely the issue of where great ideas come from. Their foundation is deep insights about customers—that part we know. But how do we get from insights to ideas? This is where we step into the process of invention and design.

"Design" is a word that we are hearing a lot in the business world these days. In the wake of Apple's demonstration of design as a source of competitive advantage, every business wants to know how to come up with its own iPod. Designers will tell you that great designs occur at the intersection of possibilities, constraints, and uncertainties. Think about those three buckets. As businesspeople, we tend to be well-versed in the identification and analysis of constraints. We have also developed fairly robust tools, such as scenario planning and options theory, for trying to deal with uncertainty writ large. But what about possibilities? If the ability to envision new possibilities lies at the heart of growth, what do we know about state-of-the-art possibility thinking? Not much, it seems, because—as we have already discussed—we have tended to see business as a largely analytic endeavor, with relatively little attention paid to its more creative aspects.

There are several places we can look for better guidance about how to develop a process for asking possibility-generating "what if?" questions. In previous chapters, we have turned to physics and biology for inspiration. Here, we'll look to engineering. Research[10] suggests that breakthrough engineering feats tend to emerge from eight different ways of illuminating new possibilities: *challenging, connecting, visualizing, collaborating, harmonizing, improvising, reorienting,* and *playing.* Let's look at how these might be applied to the search for growth.

Challenging

Challenging assumptions and defying convention are often the first steps in creative engineering. To produce something original, the engineer raises questions about the way things are done and entertains doubts about what is assumed to be necessary, natural, or customary. In the realm of business growth, we see much the same process at work when managers challenge mental models and industry assumptions. New possibilities emerge when they refuse to accept existing paradigms and constraints.

The power of mental models to block or unlock the potential to recognize opportunity is significant. Growth leaders *challenge* conventional thinking, often while *using* conventional products and existing capabilities as their starting point. The opportunities revealed when managers challenge dominant industry logic can be enormous.

Connecting

Making connections between seemingly unrelated ideas is also often at the heart of creative engineering. Novelty can result from going outside of a single field or discipline and bringing together diverse concepts, tools, capabilities, and ways of thinking. Connecting can be equally powerful in the business environment. The use of analogies that reveal similarities between different fields can provide insight into new possibilities for value creation. While adhering to the mental models of one's own industry is limiting, trying on the mental models of someone else's can surface intriguing new opportunities. Biologists talk about *exaptation*: the change in the function of a biological characteristic as the result of evolution. Those in other fields, such as business, can think of this as ideas from one area being used to solve a problem in a seemingly unrelated area. Such "borrowing" can be a source of significant opportunity.

Think of an idea as the place where nodes in a network meet: the larger and more diverse the network, the more ideas result from its myriad connections. Good ideas, Johnson argues, want to "connect, fuse, recombine—they want to reinvent themselves."[11]

Visualizing

For engineers, the first step in making something new is often thinking about how it might look—picturing it in the mind's eye. Engaging the senses beyond what words describe sometimes opens new paths to engineering creativity. Designers, we are told, "think with their pencils," allowing the emerging visual images to deepen their understanding of what they are designing as it unfolds. If managers, on the other hand, think only with their spreadsheets, how much use of imagination can we expect?

The act of creating maps and storyboards of customer experiences and interactions often triggers profoundly new insights. Presenting prototypes, no matter how rough, inspires deeper conversation. These are tools well worth adding to the manager's tool kit.

Collaborating

Many engineering innovations are the product of cooperative effort and could not be developed any other way. A group of people brings together a range of talents and capabilities, applying them to generate results that are more than the sum of the individuals' skills and creativity.

Collaboration with suppliers and customers represents one way to explore "white space" possibilities. Crossing functional and business unit boundaries can also provide rich sources for enhanced value creation. Here, tools like value chain mapping can identify both vulnerabilities and opportunities in a firm's value chain footprint.

Harmonizing

In every area of human effort, creativity is intimately associated with the quest for beauty. This is most obvious in the fine arts, but it is no less true in the practical arts like architecture and engineering. Here, especially, there is an aesthetic quality that often is about harmony, fitting the products of human ingenuity agreeably into their environment.

The origin of the word "aesthetic" is in the Greek word "aisthetikos," which means "of sense perception." Thus, we might conjecture that aesthetically pleasing ideas are those that appeal to the senses, rather than merely to cognition—new possibilities that have an *emotional* appeal, a "presence" that commands attention and invites engagement. We know that the most successful innovations combine the familiar with the novel to produce something *interesting*. Change, psychologists tell us, is primarily driven by *desire*—it is in that sense of the word "aesthetic" that we can learn from designers how to make business ideas more compelling and new possibilities more evident.

Improvising

Engineers, like most of us, are sometimes at their most creative when they are forced to be. Circumstances may require solving problems quickly or place overwhelming constraints on what seems possible. To improvise is to create "on the fly," and the results can be most ingenious.

In the business context, limitations to action are often seen as "stop signs"—as signals to give up the quest for an innovative solution. For designers, the response is the opposite—constraints act as triggers, rather than barriers, to seeing new possibilities. Some of the most successful business strategies were the result not of careful forethought but of improvisation, created out of necessity when familiar options were unavailable.

Reframing

New possibilities can emerge from new formulations of problems rather than new solutions. We have already addressed one important reframing of the question regarding customers—a move from focusing on "how do we sell the customer more of product X?" to "What need is the customer trying to satisfy?" We can also start with the specifics of the current offering and reframe from that. For example, you can take an offering that is currently commoditized and try to reframe it as a differentiated value proposition to a specific targeted audience. The following table contains seven different approaches to reframing:

Seven Questions to Reframe Your Offering

	Changing the way you see it	Strategic Questions
From	Commodity product for mass market	How can we get inside the head of individual customers?
To	Differentiated value proposition for a focused segment	
From	Customized product for single customer	How do we identify and reach a category of like-minded customers with similar needs?
To	Standardized value proposition for a larger group of customers	
From	Current product	How do we apply our expertise to problems related to the one our customers already trust us to solve?
To	Adjacent needs	
From	Stand-alone individual project	What is the outcome that customers are trying to achieve and how can we work together to help them achieve it?
To	Comprehensive multiproduct solutions	
From	Stand-alone business-unit capabilities	What can we do uniquely as a firm to leverage our capabilities across business lines to solve new needs in the marketplace?
To	White-space value propositions	
From	Stand-alone organizational capabilities	How can we use external partnering to build scale and relationships that create better value?
To	Network of capabilities	
From	Product emphasis	What is the experience that I can create of real value to customers that leverages our product expertise?
To	Service experience	

Source: From "Six Lessons to Unleash Your Inner Catalyst," *IESE Insight,* 2010, No. 6, by Jeanne Liedtka. Copyright 2010 IESE Insight. With permission of Estudios y Ediciones IESE, S.L.

Playing

Even engineers and designers do not always recognize the extent to which play contributes to creativity. Many significant technical achievements have their origins in playful experimentation. Playful engineering, as it has been called, revolves around the capacity to simulate and model wide varieties of approaches. It applies the most advanced computer modeling to facilitate enormous variation in possible forms and structures. These variations are generated by a playful approach to the problem, allowing the mind to range over possibilities that may at first glance seem unlikely or even foolish but which, through exploration, modeling, and prototyping, can become exceptional moments of creativity.

The idea of play may appear ill-suited to the business environment. After all, business is a serious endeavor. But the single-minded pursuit of efficiency and optimization can leave little room for the emergence of new possibilities—a situation that, in the long run, may cost organizations far more than some "waste" in the name of play. Play invokes a number of themes that we have already touched on. It is social, involving collaboration (or competition). It is iterative and improvisational, open to surprise and unexpected opportunities. It is also manifestly *experiential*. To play is to *try*, to *do* something instead of just thinking about it. Play does us the great service of calling attention to the value of the experiment, the willingness to forfeit certainty in the name of learning.

As we look across these eight engineering approaches to surfacing new possibilities, their applicability to finding growth is clear. Ask yourself some questions that draw on these approaches and warm up the possibility-thinking muscles of our strategic brains:

Challenging:	Take an absolute industry "truth" and turn it on its head. Ask, "What if anything were possible?" and look at the opportunities that appear.
Connecting:	Look outside the boundaries of your usual world. Ask, "What if we were operating in an industry quite different from ours—what would we be doing instead?"
Visualizing:	Put the numbers aside and get some images down on paper. Try using a napkin. What emerges?
Collaborating:	Find a partner and go forth and co-create. Ask, "What can we do together that neither of us can do alone?"
Harmonizing:	Push yourself beyond the "workable." Try to get to "intriguing." Ask, "What is really worth doing—what can I get excited about?"
Improvising:	Act as if necessity truly is the mother of invention and make surprises work for you instead of against you. Ask, "How can we turn an unexpected development into an asset?"
Reframing:	Try on a different definition of the problem. Step away from your product and ask, "What is the problem my customers are really eager to solve?"
Playing:	Go out and conduct some low-cost experiments instead of forming a committee. Ask, "What can I do today to move a new possibility forward?"

Thus far, we have talked about both the *what* and the *how* of idea generation. We'd like to conclude this chapter by turning our attention to the *who*. Because the key here is to gather as rich a trove of ideas as possible, the search for great growth ideas must come from many sources throughout the organization.

Growth Roles and Responsibilities

One of our themes thus far in this book has been the need to involve *all* employees, at every level, in the search for growth. Senior managers identify areas of opportunity to play in and set the rules for how the rest of the organization will look for them. Frontline employees tap into the local knowledge of customers. Middle managers devote time and attention to designing the kind of research that produces deep customer insight. P&L leaders create diverse teams to carry ideas into the experimentation phase.

At Senior Levels

We have already talked about the responsibility of senior leaders to establish an aligned system that supports their growth ambitions. Another responsibility is elucidating the boundaries within which the rest of the organization will be encouraged to join in the search for opportunities.

In thinking about setting the strategic themes that define those boundaries, there has been a shift from a belief that senior executives can predict and control the future of their industries to a widespread acknowledgement that "the future," as a single point estimate, is not predictable and that many serious management errors have occurred when strategies and plans were tied to a set of assumptions about the future that later proved to be wrong. Scholars Gary Hamel and C.K. Prahalad developed the concept of "strategic intent" to represent the presence of a highly visible direction for the future. This intent sets the boundaries for organizational action, but does not specify particular actions to be taken within them. In doing so, it achieves coherence and focus while freeing the rest of the organization to respond to emerging opportunities:

> Strategic intent also implies a particular point of view about the long-term market or competitive position that a firm hopes to build over the coming decade or so. Hence, it conveys a *sense of direction*. A strategic intent is differentiated; it implies a competitively unique point of view about the future. It holds out to employees the promise of exploring new competitive territory. Hence, it conveys a *sense of discovery*. Strategic intent has an emotional edge to it; it is a goal that employees perceive as inherently worthwhile. Hence, it implies a *sense of destiny*. Direction, discovery, and destiny. These are the attributes of strategic intent.[12]

Strategic intent provides the focus that allows individuals within an organization to marshal and leverage their energy, to focus attention, to resist distraction, and to concentrate for as long as it takes to achieve a goal. In the disorienting swirl of change, such psychic energy may well be the most scarce resource an organization has, and only those who utilize it most efficiently will succeed. But within this intent-driven focus, there must be room for intelligent opportunism that not only furthers intended strategy but also allows for the emergence of new strategies. Leaders need to establish a shared vocabulary and purpose *and* an openness to dissent and diverging views.

Urban Outfitters, a leading specialty retailer, provides a case in point about the role of strategic themes in setting the boundaries for growth. Two core beliefs shape the company's view of the opportunities it is interested in pursuing. The first is that scarcity creates demand. "We never want to do a Starbucks and become ubiquitous" is how CEO Glen Senk described the philosophy.[13] The second is the belief "that we must control the customer experience." These two beliefs are reflected in Urban's newest business, BHLDN (pronounced "beholden"), a bridal boutique for the edgy crowd, filling what has been seen as a significant gap in the bridal market. It provides merchandise (beyond dresses) for the complete bridal experience and has that signature Urban sense of personal connection.

Having set the themes that bound growth interests, senior leaders have a responsibility to put in place systems that invite, capture, and catalog ideas from both employees and customers.

Throughout the Organization

Few organizations communicate a clear message that what frontline employees observe and learn is important. Even fewer have put in place a systematic process for tapping into what they know. This is the low-hanging fruit of growth.

Scholars studying the broader inclusion of managers in idea generation have noted a number of significant advantages. As the pace of change accelerates, it becomes more difficult for senior managers to adequately monitor, interpret, and respond to environmental change; those closest to the customer are likely to have access to the most valuable local knowledge. Intelligently opportunistic behavior on the part of lower-level managers leaves an organization less dependent on the prescience of its senior managers. Contributing to the development of ideas can be energizing and fulfilling. And the bifurcation of formulation and implementation activities masks the payoffs of investing time in consensual decision making. Thus, inclusion is seen as having the potential to produce better, more implementable solutions to which managers are more committed. Yet, it is important to recognize that inclusion has long been seen as having serious pitfalls as well as benefits.

The following arguments have been offered against more widespread inclusion of lower-level managers in idea generation: (1) only corporate management has a sufficiently broad overview and is able to exercise emotional detachment from particular ideas; (2) soliciting a manager's viewpoint, but then disregarding it, can have a negative effect on the manager's motivation; and (3) there is not enough time for all managers to participate.

According to those arguments, successful inclusive processes rely on (1) managers who bring an institutional view to the process, to prevent discussions from deteriorating into parochial wrangling; (2) decision-making processes in which people feel they have a real voice and which they see as legitimate and valuable even when they produce outcomes different from those that managers initially propose; (3) efficient processes capable of involving large numbers of people without collapsing under their own weight; and (4) outcomes that frontline employees see as clear, compelling, and "salient," whose underlying rationale they understand and support.

An individual's decision to share his or her information and perspectives is a complex one. It requires a relationship between leaders and members characterized by trust and a willingness to listen and to make one's logic explicit and open to self-examination. It also requires an environment of psychological safety, clarity around purpose, and a sense of urgency about the future. These

Crowdsourcing

In today's web-enabled environment, no discussion of idea generation would be complete without a nod to the phenomenon of crowdsourcing, the online distributed solicitation of ideas and solutions. From the creation of tournaments aimed at soliciting solutions from outside experts to complicated technical problems in industries like pharmaceuticals to the request for new-product ideas from customers though websites like Dell's IdeaStorm, Crowdsourcing is everywhere. Researchers have demonstrated that the quality, originality, and feasibility of ideas offered by users can exceed that of a firm's own professional staff.[14]

Like so much else we have talked about in these pages, crowdsourcing's value seems to lie in the diversity of the crowd.

Is Crowdsourcing the silver bullet that solves the idea generation problem? We think not and would not want to put our eggs in that basket at the expense of doing the kind of rich discovery research on customers' unarticulated needs that we have talked about here. It is, however, another arrow in the quiver in the search for new ideas—one especially fitted to the social networking world we live in today—and cannot be ignored.

requirements fall squarely within the responsibility of senior managers, who must model and reward the appropriate behaviors, as we noted in Chapter 3.

The kind of employee engagement that mobilizes an organization's front line to find growth requires asking employees to bring more than just data and opinions to the process—it seeks to find what energizes them, and constructs the strategic intent itself around that set of possibilities.

And so, through the process of discovery, managers have learned a great deal about the lives of the people they hope to serve. The organization has invited the contribution of both its employees and customers. Through brainstorming and concept development, some concepts have emerged that have the potential to create value for customers while meeting organizational objectives. Now it is time to make hard choices, identifying the best concepts in order to guide innovation efforts and further investment decisions. It is time to construct a set of small experiments, the topic of our next chapter.

5

Learning Launches

Doing Growth Experiments

In previous chapters, we have discussed how growth is enabled by individual and organizational mindsets, an internal Growth System, and systematic processes to identify growth opportunities. After identifying growth opportunities, what do we do next? How do we evaluate which ones are worth investment?

Not a Business Plan

First, let's discuss what most companies do but you should not. In most companies, growth ideas are prematurely funneled into a process that requires developing a formal business plan before any genuine evaluation takes place. Usually, that business plan is based on financial projections generated to demonstrate that the growth idea can meet the business's needed return on investment (ROI) hurdle. Because many growth ideas are new, historical data do not exist. Without history, one then has to guess—yes, make guesses—about the viability of the new idea in order to prepare the business plan and demonstrate, on paper at least, an acceptable rate of return. Developing a full business plan as a first step in evaluating growth ideas is problematic. It requires managers to make a series of more-or-less educated guesses without experience or data. This is a risky and flawed process. We think there is a better way to evaluate growth ideas. That method is a Learning Launch: a low-cost and time-efficient method of conducting a series of small experiments to test growth ideas and the assumptions on which they are based.

Tyranny of Analysis and ROI

Conducting a Learning Launch differs significantly from making a business plan. Using a business plan process with inadequate data is what we call the "tyranny of analysis and ROI." Managers spend considerable time preparing these plans, making presentations, and getting approvals that effectively serve little purpose. In addition, in many cases that process creates unrealistic expectations and leads to premature emotional buy-in to untested ideas. It also can strengthen cognitive biases that make it difficult to see and process disconfirming facts—the facts that indicate the new idea is not really viable. Relying on a business plan too early in the development of a growth idea often results in decisions based on educated guesses or "fudged" assumptions geared toward hitting an internal investment hurdle. This is a crazy way to run a railroad.

Premature Anointing of "Needle Movers"

Doing a business plan prematurely can produce another negative consequence. Sometimes, in choosing among competing growth ideas without adequate data, senior managers become enamored with an idea that they think can be a "big needle mover." When that happens, it can be difficult to kill those ideas if they prove to be not as good as hoped. It is hard to call one's own baby ugly. So hard, in fact, that we know of many cases where growth ideas that should have been killed were nonetheless funded for years, albeit in declining amounts, because of the reluctance of senior management to admit failure.

Senior management is always looking for those "needle movers"—the next big hit. This mentality can result in a growth strategy of making a few large bets. We think a better strategy at this stage is to make many small bets and defer the needle-mover process until you have more and better data.

Growth Ideas Are Just Ideas

In most cases, a growth idea is just that—an idea, hunch, intuition, or educated guess. Growth ideas are based on implicit, usually unstated, assumptions about the market, customer needs, the business's capability to execute, and how easy it would be to defend the idea from competitors' challenges. Assumptions about these variables should be tested. At this stage, it is premature to put untested assumptions through a business plan process. Rather, they need to be put through an evidence-gathering process to test the commercial viability of the underlying assumptions.

This does not mean you never do a business plan with financial projections. The question is one of timing. What we recommend is deferring the business plan process until you have better data to justify the assumptions necessary to do projected ROI computations. Finding better data to support or refute your assumptions is more valuable than fudging assumptions so that your business plan can meet the needed investment return hurdle.

Not a New-Product Rollout

A Learning Launch also differs from a traditional new-product rollout. At this early stage, all you have is a growth idea—that is, a new product you think customers need and would pay for. Many companies believe that having an idea about customer needs is the same as knowing customers will buy the new product, and so they move directly to a product rollout process. Product rollouts generally require a large investment of people, time, and money to create the product that engineers or marketing people *think* customers need. Rolling out a new product with limited information is a huge and risky bet. Again, we think that it is less risky to first get more and better data upon which to make that major investment decision.

So, a Learning Launch differs from both a traditional business plan process and a traditional product rollout process. What, then, is a Learning Launch?

A Learning Launch Is a Small, Low-Cost Experiment

A Learning Launch is a small, fast, low-cost experiment designed to gather data you can use to make an informed decision about the potential viability of a growth idea. Learning Launches are intended to help you make evidence-based investment decisions. A Learning Launch process often results in a series of iterative Learning Launches, each building upon the information learned from previous ones. You may do three or four small, low-cost Learning Launches on the same idea before making the big decision whether to fund continued development of the idea or to drop it and invest elsewhere.

In Chapter 1, we used the analogy that successful business growth is like winning at craps in Las Vegas. Professional players place many small bets and adapt and learn as they go. Likewise, we talked about how professional venture capital investors make big winning investments only around 20 percent of the time. Picking winners at the growth idea stage is also a low-probability game. Because most growth ideas fail to produce a big win, there should be a more efficient, faster, and less expensive way to test them. The Learning Launch process will produce better data, efficiently, to make better investment decisions.

Let's say that you have a growth idea. You think it is a good idea or you would not have suggested it. But it is an educated guess at best that the idea has genuine growth potential. There are many unknowns that translate to uncertainties and risks. A Learning Launch approach is intended to systematically reduce unknowns. Learning Launches require you to unpack and define the critical assumptions that underlie your growth idea. For example, what do you think the real customer need is? How do you know that? Why are current offerings (yours and your competitors') not meeting that need? Why do you think you can meet that need? By clearly identifying your assumptions, you can find data to test their validity.

Being a Good Detective

Learning Launches require a detective's mentality. While you may be too young to remember the hit TV police detective show *Dragnet,* it is illustrative because Detective Joe Friday often said, "Just the facts, ma'am!" That is the attitude you need to do a Learning Launch. The goal of a Learning Launch is to get better evidence so that you can critically assess your idea. The goal is *not* to prove you have a good idea. This is a significant point. Why? Because if you undertake to prove that your idea is a good one, then your search, investigation, and processing of information are more likely to be biased toward supporting your idea. Your findings will be unreliable because of your confirmation bias, and that bias can lead your business down a costly path. The process is not a Confirmation Launch. It is a Learning Launch.

A Search for "Truth"

Learning Launches are a business application of the scientific method. Learning Launches require a scientist's method of following the facts wherever they may lead. Recall the discussion in Chapter 3 about the organizational mindset of critical inquiry and challenging underlying assumptions. That is what a Learning Launch experiment is meant to do—find the big, faulty assumption behind your growth idea. If you adopt an unbiased approach of critical inquiry, you will either find evidence to support a growth idea or save your company valuable time and money, allowing those resources to be allocated to more worthy growth ideas. If you learn important information about an idea, then a Learning Launch is not a failure because you can either amend your idea or drop it and move on to test others.

Evidence-Based Management

Another way to understand the purpose of a Learning Launch comes from the vice president of engineering for product development at one of our consulting clients. Quite frankly, this individual did not get Learning Launches the first three times we discussed the process with him. He understood that his boss, the president of the business unit, loved the methodology and wanted it implemented in the business. We decided to give it one more try. While having dinner with the VP and one of his senior managers, we again tried to differentiate the Learning Launch process from the traditional business plan process of assessing new ideas. Understand that he had used the business plan process to evaluate new growth ideas for years. At one point in our discussion, however, he spontaneously said, "I get it. Why didn't you just tell me that a Learning Launch is an evidence-based management tool to be used to get better evidence to make better investment decisions?"

Precisely. From that night on, we have used his evidence-based management explanation to describe the Learning Launch process—doing experiments to test the critical underlying assumptions of a growth idea in a low-cost, rapid way to gather evidence to make better investment decisions.

Low-Cost Learning

Most growth ideas are based on many assumptions or educated guesses. Testing them all simultaneously would be time consuming and costly. A key objective of the Learning Launch process is to facilitate rapid and low-cost learning. Because a Learning Launch is an iterative learning process, one can start by testing a new idea's most critical assumptions—the assumptions that if disconfirmed would require dropping the idea or making major changes to it.

So we are looking for a relatively quick assessment by focusing first on foundational assumptions: For this idea to be viable, what assumptions must be true?

The low-cost feature of this process comes from the studies of successful serial entrepreneurs. Contrary to popular belief, they are not big risk takers with new ideas. Instead, they place small bets—bets that have acceptable costs or losses if they do not pan out.

The idea is to learn in a relatively low-cost way so you can test many potentially good ideas. Remember, if you generate 1,000 growth ideas and choose 100 of those ideas to test with Learning Launches, you can expect 10 or so to prove worthy of further exploration. You want to learn quickly and cheaply so that you can conduct a large number of Learning Launches from which you will identify a small number of ideas worthy of further investment.

By adopting characteristics of both a detective and a scientist, you are ready to begin the search for better evidence about the worthiness of your idea. For the purpose of our discussion, we are assuming you are doing an initial Learning Launch on a new offering for an external customer. However, the Learning Launch methodology can also be used for new offerings for internal customers: Many companies use Learning Launches to test business process improvements, new organizational structures, new measurement systems, and other internal improvements.

How to Do a Learning Launch

The Learning Launch process involves eight steps:

1. Turning your growth idea into a hypothesis that can be tested
2. Creating the right team to do the Learning Launch
3. Unpacking or defining the assumptions underlying your idea
4. Prioritizing those assumptions
5. Designing a test for each prioritized assumption
6. Doing the tests
7. Managing the Learning Launch process
8. Making a decision: Continue exploration, move to development, or drop the idea

Over the last four years, we have worked with many companies on the design of over 200 Learning Launches. What have we learned? First, we have learned that the Learning Launch process requires a different way of thinking for most businesspeople, especially those working in product-centric companies. Like anything new, it takes practice to become good at the process. Second, companies report that experience with the systematic analytical processes involved in evaluating new ideas through Learning Launches can enhance critical thinking more broadly. Here is a chart of the process:

Learning Launch Process

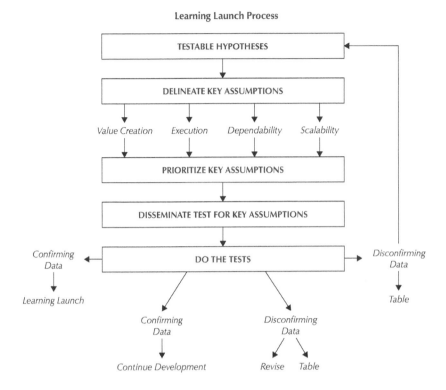

Step 1—Creating a Testable Hypothesis

A growth idea needs to be specific enough to test. In many cases, that means transforming it into a testable hypothesis. That requires translating a big, dreamy idea about a new product or solution into a narrower and testable business idea. That narrower, testable idea must identify a specific set of customers who have a specific problem that you hypothesize can be solved with a specific idea better than the solutions offered by the competition.

The testable hypothesis format is this: This new idea can solve this problem (or provide this needed value) to these specific customers better than the competitor's product or service because of these reasons. The information you gather will either support or refute this hypothesis.

Concretely developing a testable hypothesis often proves difficult for first-time users of the Learning Launch methodology. The tighter and more specific the hypothesis, the more easily testable it is. To facilitate thinking concretely about what you must prove (or not), we have found the concept of the "elevator pitch" to be helpful. This means you should transform your idea into a business concept that you can explain to a third party in the time it takes to ride an elevator from the fifth floor of a building to the first floor. To do that, your elevator pitch must meet the 3Cs—that is, it must be concrete, clear, and concise. We have found the following questions useful:

1. What is the specific problem?
2. Who specifically has this problem?
3. How will we propose to solve the problem?
4. How is our solution better than existing solutions?

Step 2—Creating the Right Team

The purpose of a Learning Launch is to gather data to assess the validity of critical assumptions underlying a growth idea. In this search, it must be stressed that finding disconfirming data is as important as finding confirming data. For example, you need to know as early as possible whether your idea is one that customers are not willing to pay for since their need is not strong enough. However, it is sometimes the case that enthusiasm for an idea biases the gathering and evaluation of data. This can lead to costly mistakes and wasted time. Being attentive to disconfirming data requires one to proactively mitigate the risks of cognitive blindness and cognitive dissonance.

Cognitive Risks

There are at least two cognitive risks that can interfere with gathering and evaluating data about a new idea—cognitive blindness and cognitive dissonance. While similar in results—both interfere with an objective assessment of a new idea—they differ somewhat in how their effects must be mitigated. First, we will discuss these cognitive risks. Then, we will discuss ways to mitigate them.

Cognitive Blindness   We know from psychology and neuroscience research that our brains often fail to process information we see, hear, or read that disagrees with or fails to fit into our existing views about the world—including our business world. You cannot prevent this. It is how our brains work. This is called cognitive blindness. We all have mental models or constructs of our industry, business model, products, and customers. Generally, we prefer data that fit best with our past experiences, mental models, and beliefs. Cognitive blindness to data that materially differ from these experiences, mental models, and beliefs obstructs an objective evaluation of new ideas.

We all can fall prey to cognitive biases, which can result in cognitive blindness. These biases distort our processing and interpreting of information. If the growth idea is yours or one you particularly like, you will be naturally biased to prove that it is a good one. Although subconscious, confirmation bias makes you more likely to miss, misinterpret, rationalize, or devalue disconfirming data than a more objective person would be. This is a natural bias, but it is not good if we are looking for the truth.

Unless you work to mitigate the risks of cognitive blindness, it will reduce the likelihood that the growth idea will receive an unbiased evaluation.

Cognitive Dissonance   The brain is a beautiful system—it operates on the principle of not having a single point of failure. By that we mean that even if disconfirming information gets past your cognitive blindness mechanism, your brain tends to de-emphasize the difference. This minimization of the difference or the discounting of the importance of disconfirming data is called cognitive dissonance.

Create the Team—The Right Team

So how do you mitigate these cognitive risks? Notice, we did not say eliminate them. That is not possible. They are part of every human being. There are, however, steps you can take to minimize their effects.

You mitigate the cognitive risks of distorting the data by creating a team to do the Learning Launch experiment. Not just any team, but the right kind of team, made up of people with different experiences, points of view, and expertise. We've already seen, in Chapter 2, how team diversity can compensate for managers with narrow repertoires. Diversity also increases the probability that disconfirming data will be recognized by at least one team member. Our experience suggests that you should have at least four but not more than five people on the team. They should have a range of functional expertise (such as manufacturing, research, marketing, sales, and customer service). Gender diversity and different industry experience are also helpful. The team should include at least two people who were not involved in the creation of the idea and one member who is skeptical of it. Every team filled with high Ds (whom we learned about in Chapter 2) needs at least one high C member—someone with a "prevention" orientation who can balance the "promoters," who have a bias for action.

Having people with different backgrounds increases the likelihood that disconfirming data will be recognized because those people will have different areas of cognitive blindness. Having a skeptic on the team also increases the chance of disconfirming data being recognized. To the skeptic, disconfirming data often are confirming data. The skeptic thought it was a weak idea to begin with. Diversity of backgrounds and diversity of emotional buy-in to the idea both help mitigate cognitive risks.

Usually the person who generated the growth idea will view the skeptic, initially, as a killjoy. However, by the end of the Learning Launch process, the skeptic usually is considered a valuable asset because he or she has improved the assessment. The skeptic asks the tough questions that ultimately a senior manager would likely ask. No idea is perfect. All have issues or risks. It is better to illuminate them up front and directly than to pretend none exist. Having a skeptic on the team will help you do that.

As we will see later, defining what data would be disconfirming to your key assumptions prior to gathering any data will also help the team know what to look for and mitigate biases.

Step 3—Unpacking or Defining Key Assumptions

You have a growth idea. You think it is good. You have assembled the right team to conduct the Learning Launch experiment. How do you test the idea? What data do you need to find that will reduce the unknowns? To determine the data you need, you first have to unpack and illuminate the key assumptions underlying your growth idea. This unpacking process is like peeling away the prickly leaves of an artichoke until you get to the heart of the matter. You "peel the artichoke" by using a technique called the "5 Whats," which is nothing more than a continuous process of asking, "What must be true for a statement to be true?" You can also ask "5 Whys" repeatedly to get to the foundation of why you think something may be true. The point is that your questioning must be continuous.

This unpacking process is applied to the testing of four kinds of assumptions. We start with assumptions about customers' needs. Then we move to assumptions about how the business can meet those needs—execution assumptions. Then we come to assumptions about how our way of meeting those needs will be competitively defensible. Last, we unpack our assumptions about why we think a large number of potential customers have similar needs. We call these four tests

- Customer Value (Needs) Test
- Execution Test
- Defensibility Test
- Scaling Test

These tests seek to answer the questions:

- Do customers really value or need our offering?
- Can we do it?
- Will competitors quickly be able to do it, too?
- Do a large number of customers have this need?

Unpacking assumptions is a challenging process to learn. Our experience is that it generally takes more than six hours to do this well the first time and works best in shorter sessions over a couple of days.

The Customer Value (Needs) Test

Many companies with a new-product idea start by asking, "Can we build it?" Underlying that question may be the assumptions that "if we build good products, customers will buy them" or "we know what customers need because we are the product experts." Too often, these assumptions prove false.

We recommend that every Learning Launch start with customers. We are devotees of Peter Drucker's statement that the "ultimate purpose of a business" is to "create a customer."[1]

The Customer Value (Needs) Test focuses on needs rather than wants. What is the specific customer need our idea can solve? What is the customer problem? Customer needs for this test are "got to haves" not "nice to haves." Customers are more likely to spend money to meet compelling needs, to solve major problems, and to relieve a big "pain" than they are to buy products or services that would be just "nice to have." Another way to look at customer needs is to ask, "Why will the customer think we are adding value with this idea?"

Understanding customer needs requires putting yourself in the customer's shoes and viewing value from a customer's perspective, not your own. The critical question to answer is, "What is the need and how do we *know* that the customer has this need?" Are you assuming customer need without evidence that it exists?

You can unpack the customer needs assumptions underlying your growth idea by using the following questions as prompts:

1. Who is the customer?
2. What is the customer need?
3. How do we know the customer has this need?
4. How important is it for the customer to meet or solve this need?
5. How big is the need?

6. How time sensitive is the need?
7. How urgently does the customer want to meet this need?
8. How does the growth idea meet that need?
9. Do customers have money allocated to meet this need?
10. Who makes the buying decision?
11. Who influences or has to concur with the buying decision?

So, you have to "peel the artichoke" until you get to the heart of the matter by constantly asking, "What has to be true for this statement to be true?," "Why?," and "How do we know?" You must drill down to what you think the answers are to those questions. After uncovering your assumptions, however, your analysis is not over. Your assumptions about customer needs must be tested.

The end result of this questioning process should be a list of assumptions stated in simple sentence form. For example, "Our customers need a quicker way to do X." You will most likely have a long list of simple statements to test.

The Cop-Outs

Sometimes a person with an idea discounts the value of getting direct data about customer needs. In addition, he or she may have trouble articulating the real need. When challenged about his or her reluctance to go to the customer to get data, there are two common responses. The first is to devalue the customer while inflating one's wisdom. That response goes something like this: "Most customers do not know what needs they have. So it is a waste of time to ask them." The second is to assume the new product will create customer demand. Here, the rationale goes like this: "A customer need does not have to exist, because we can create needs." Both responses should be dismissed. We don't intend merely to ask them if they would buy; we want to see some skin in the game. Getting accurate information about customer needs is critical to a Learning Launch.

Gauging customer needs, however, is not always straightforward. We know that traditional market studies and focus group techniques are not highly reliable. In Chapter 4 we discussed techniques and processes to understand customer needs even when the customer cannot initially verbalize them. Those techniques involve interacting with actual or potential customers on their own terms in their own environments. Understanding customer needs requires interaction with the ultimate customer—the end user. Observing customers and asking questions about the job they are trying to accomplish is a start.

As an example, on a recent Learning Launch a client went into the field three times to talk to end users of a product. From those conversations our client learned that the customer need was sharply different than what he had assumed. Moreover, the client learned what changes to the product the end user would value the most. Assumptions about customer needs are risky. Sometimes neither you nor the customer can articulate or even identify the actual need without direct interaction and questioning. Like the Learning Launch process generally, the Customer Value (Needs) Test is often an iterative process in which both you and the customer develop an understanding of what the need is and how you might be able to address it.

Note that we have heard the example of Apple creating customer needs hundreds of times. We fundamentally reject the proposition that Apple created needs. Instead, we believe the underlying needs existed and that Apple creatively designed products to meet them better than anyone else. Of course, years ago if Apple had asked consumers whether they needed an iPod or iPhone or iPad, they would have most likely said no. But what Apple did was to meet consumers' emotional and functional needs by designing products that were compellingly different from the competition's. Apple did this through its combination of design, beauty, ease of use, and functionality. It met underlying needs. It did not create needs.

The Execution Test

The Execution Test asks how you can meet those customer needs. Do you have the capabilities to do what is required? Do you need to buy or build capabilities? Do you need to partner with others?

The Execution Test is easier than the Customer Value (Needs) Test because it focuses on understanding what your business can and cannot do. The following questions will help you unpack critical execution assumptions that need testing:

1. What solution meets the needs of the customer?
2. Do we have the capabilities to produce the solution?
3. Do we have the capabilities to market, deliver, and service the solution?
4. What capabilities are missing?
5. Where do we get the missing capabilities?
6. Which value chain partners or suppliers are critical to the solution?
7. Can they and will they meet our needs?

8. Can we meet the customer's needs at a cost/price that creates value for both the customer and us?

At the end of this questioning process, you should have a list of execution assumptions transformed into simple hypotheses that can be tested. For example, you may assume that you can meet the customer's needs at a cost and price that is value creating for both the customer and for your business. But how do you know this? Your testable hypotheses are: You can build the needed product at $X. The customer will pay that price for the product. At that price, you can make an acceptable net profit. At that price, the customer perceives good value. You need to systematically gather data to test whether these are true.

The Defensibility Test

The purpose of generating growth ideas is to create a pipeline of growth experiments. A robust pipeline of growth ideas will funnel down into a smaller number of Learning Launch experiments, which will produce a yet smaller number of growth initiatives that will move into a Growth Portfolio (Chapter 6) for funding and further development. The ultimate goal of these Growth Processes (Chapters 4-6) is to produce new streams of revenue that will replace a business's declining revenue streams.

To create a new revenue stream, a growth idea must have the potential to be sustainable in a large enough marketplace for a long enough period of time. That period of time will depend on the velocity of change and the product life cycle in your industry. For example, product life cycles in the automobile industry are generally much longer than those in the consumer electronics industry. To be sustainable in your industry, a new growth idea must also maintain a reasonable level of profitability, which means that you must be able to defend your market position against competitors.

The Defensibility Test requires you to acknowledge that your idea is probably not unique. In addition, absent legally protected intellectual property, it is unlikely that you have capabilities that competitors cannot replicate or reverse engineer. So the issue addressed by the Defensibility Test is broader than "Do you have or will you have competition?" The question also is one of time—"How much time will you have in the marketplace with your new idea before you have competition?" and "Can you maintain acceptable profit margins when you have competition?" Remember from Chapter 1 that a high-margin new product is like food to foraging ants. The ants, in the form of competitors, will come.

The following questions are helpful in thinking about your defensibility assumptions:

1. Which competitors are currently offering a solution to this specific customer need?
2. Why are their offerings not meeting the need?
3. Do our existing competitors have the capabilities to offer our solution?
4. Are there companies that now serve these customers in other ways that could attempt to meet this need?
5. Are there companies that have the capabilities to meet this need but are not now focusing on this customer segment?
6. How long do we think it would take our competitors to build or buy the capabilities to meet the need?
7. How would we defend our margins when competition comes?

At the end of this process, you should have a list of defensibility assumptions to test. The next test goes to the issue of market size. Can your growth idea scale? How many customers have or will have this need?

Scalability Test

Notice that we put the Scalability Test last. Many managers want to know at the idea generation stage whether an idea could be a "big needle mover." This mentality carries over from the traditional business plan process of prematurely doing ROI computations to assess a new idea. We put the Scalability Test last because gathering evidence about scalability requires a better understanding of customer needs as well as an ability both to execute and defend against competition. Assessing scalability is important, but like calculating ROI, it is important to do at the appropriate time.

Questions to help you think about scalability assumptions are:

1. How many different customers have this need?
2. How often does this need arise?
3. What are the risks that this need will not exist in the future?
4. What are the risks that this need may be met in the future by new technology?
5. Are there different customer segments that might have this need?
6. Can our solution be "downsized" and offered at a much lower price to a different customer segment?

7. Can the solution be combined with other solutions to offer a compelling macro-solution to a large number of customers?

At the end of Step 3 in the Learning Launch process, you should have a long list of concrete assumptions grouped by the four test categories. The next step is to prioritize those assumptions by deciding which ones, if disconfirming data are found, would require major amendments to the idea or dropping the idea altogether.

Learning Launches are meant to be an iterative, incremental learning process. You will probably do several Learning Launches in succession on the same idea because what you learn on the first Learning Launch may require you to adjust or create new testable assumptions or amend your proposed solution. What you learn from an initial Learning Launch may also send you in a direction you had not considered previously.

Step 4—Prioritizing Your Key Assumptions

You may think prioritizing your key assumptions is easy, but it usually is not. A couple of dynamics come into play. First, individual team members tend to think that the assumptions they generated are the most important. Second, if the company is product-centric, team members usually want to focus on execution assumptions because they know more about making products. They may think they know better than customers how to solve customer needs. We call this "product arrogance."

Third, after spending hours unpacking assumptions, team members often have a pent-up demand for doing a test, and that can inhibit the critical thinking and debate necessary to select foundational, mission-critical assumptions. Think of a stone wall. Which stones are so foundational that if you removed them the entire wall would crumble?

Keep in mind that a Learning Launch should be designed to be a quick and low-cost experiment. The first one should focus on key customer needs and execution assumptions. Then, as you learn more, the next Learning Launch can include defensibility and scaling assumptions. Why do we recommend starting with the critical assumptions about customer needs and execution? Until you understand the need, you cannot assess whether you can meet it. And, until you have more evidence about the need and how your business would meet it, you cannot realistically explore the defensibility or scalability of your solution.

We recommend that you prioritize your customer needs assumptions and execution assumptions. Then select the most critical ones that, if disconfirmed, would require you to drop the idea. Of course, if you have knowledge of a competitor that is already delivering or developing solutions to these needs, then you should gather that evidence, too. Be practical and fact based. Generally, focusing on customer needs first works best, but there is no single approach to prioritizing either the tests or their assumptions. It all depends on the idea and the context.

Step 5 — Designing the Test for Each Assumption

Designing the test for each assumption should answer the questions *who, what, where,* and *when.*

Who will look for *what* data *where* and *when?*

The following is a template for designing tests of assumptions. These questions can be used to create process forms for each assumption to be tested.

Assumption Test Design Template

Purpose   A Learning Launch is a learning process. It is a discovery and testing process. Its purpose is to find the "truth," whatever that may be. Its purpose is not to prove that the idea is good. Its purpose is to find enough high-quality confirming and disconfirming evidence that a review committee has enough data on which to base an investment decision. Your team should work as hard at finding disconfirming data as it does at finding confirming data. A Learning Launch requires critical inquiry, constructive debate, and the mentality of a relentless detective searching for the facts.

Process: Discovery Planning

1. State the assumption to be tested.
2. What facts do we already know that confirm the assumption?
3. What facts do we already know that cast doubt on the assumption?
4. What additional facts would confirm the assumption?
5. What additional facts would disconfirm the assumption?
6. For each fact that would confirm: How will we learn those facts?
   a. Who knows those facts?
   b. Where do we find those facts?
   c. How will the evidence be gathered? Who? Where? When?
   d. How many different sources do we need?
   e. How have we mitigated confirmation bias?

7. For each fact that would disconfirm: How will we learn those facts?

    a. Who knows those facts?

    b. Where do we find those facts?

    c. How will the evidence be gathered? Who? Where? When?

    d. How many different sources do we need?

    e. How have we mitigated confirmation bias?

Now you are ready to go forth and gather evidence.

Step 6—Doing the Test: Gathering the Data

Testing your assumptions about a new idea requires project management, interviewing, listening, and evaluation skills. Much of the data will be gathered through interviews and evidentiary research. There is both an art and a science to good discovery interviewing. A good way to learn how to conduct discovery interviews is to look at legal training materials on asking discovery deposition questions. After gaining some understanding of the customer's needs, the next step is engaging the customer in "co-creating" a rudimentary solution. This may be in the form of an initial prototype. The key is to continually engage the customer in creating the needed solution.

Some Best Practices

As a general rule, at least two people should attend every discovery interview. For critical interviews, having the skeptic attend is advisable. Likewise, you need a process similar to the U.S. Army's After Action Review, in which the interviewing team meets immediately after the interview to critique and document the review. The documentation should record all differences among team members about what was heard.

In conducting interviews and searching for documentation, remember the goal: the facts. The quality of the evidence you discover will be directly related to the quality of the questions you ask and the quality of your document search parameters. You want to "peel the artichoke" and use the "5 Whats" or the "5 Whys" questioning techniques that you used to unpack your assumptions here. This process is made easier by preparing a short list of questions to be used consistently in interviewing people about the same points. And you want to have a short list of questions designed to discover disconfirming evidence.

Recently, we worked on the design of a Learning Launch with a communications equipment manufacturer. In a meeting after the team's first discovery expedition, team members reported that they talked to Mr. X, who said there was the need for the new product idea. They said it was a short customer interview. When we asked why they had not drilled down deeper to understand the reasons for the customer's stated need, how important the need was, whether Mr. X had buying authority, and whether money was available to meet that need, the team's answer was, "Mr. X confirmed the need." We then asked who else they'd talked to, and they said, "No one," because Mr. X answered their question. Team members not only failed to ask key questions, but also failed to interview more than one individual about the customer's needs. In this case, confirmation bias overwhelmed true discovery.

Discovery requires persistent curiosity. You should pursue the same facts different ways. You should ask different questions that would elicit the same confirming or disconfirming evidence. In interviewing customers, you should ask as many questions as possible to understand their needs. After you think you understand the need, verbalize your understanding to the interviewees and ask them to add, modify, or change your statement to clearly represent their need. Once you have explored the customer need, engage the customer in a discussion of possible solutions.

Exploring possible solutions with the customer has two benefits. First, it will deepen your understanding of the need. Second, the customer becomes emotionally invested in trying to help you create a solution.

The discovery process is different from a sales process. Learning Launches require listening and exploration to determine a customer need and possible solutions. As such, you do not want to jump quickly to a sales mode. When you are selling, you are not listening, and you are probably leading the witness. In addition, you do not yet have enough information to develop a product to address the client need—you are using only a rough prototype.

Documentation of your data gathering is critical. One person should always take notes that are as complete as possible. Information that seems unimportant initially may become very important after further information gathering.

The best practices for doing the test described in this section are not meant to be exhaustive. We recommend that Learning Launch teams create their own best practices list. Those lists could be posted on a company Growth Processes website to be shared and improved upon by others.

Step 7—Managing the Learning Launch Process

Managing or overseeing a Learning Launch takes project management, critical thinking, creativity, and constructive debate skills. It is part process and part art.

Managing a Learning Launch includes both process and quality control functions. The more inexperienced the team is in doing a Learning Launch, the more frequently the Learning Launch must be monitored and reviewed. Generally, we recommend weekly meetings with a process review, a data review, and a discussion about the quality of the data and the interpretation. In each weekly meeting, the team manager must remember to focus on disconfirming data and whether the search for such data is as aggressive as the search for confirming data.

Weekly reviews, invariably, will adjust the priority of assumptions to test and often require adapting the idea and the assumptions. Again, a Learning Launch is an iterative, incremental learning process. The weekly reviews ensure that teams are taking into account what they should be learning. Learning from the data the team has collected can change ideas, assumptions, and how assumptions should be tested. In some cases, new information can send teams off for discovery in a completely new direction. Think of feedback loops or a zig-zag learning process rather than straight-line learning. These review meetings are not short. Until the team learns how to use the Learning Launch process effectively, these reviews can take hours each week.

As the team gathers data about the critical customer needs and execution assumptions, it should in succeeding weeks look at critical defensibility and scaling assumptions.

At some point, the manager and the team will decide either to drop the idea or to seek further funding to explore or develop it. If the team seeks further funding, we are assuming that a high-level review committee must approve the funding.

Step 8—Making a Decision: Continue Exploration, Move to Development, or Drop

At some point in a Learning Launch, the moment will come when you must decide whether to continue exploration, move to development, or drop the idea. Remember, as important as finding a good idea is weeding out the not-so-good ones. Perhaps 1,000 growth ideas will generate 100 Learning Launches, which may result in 10 growth initiatives to be placed in a Growth Portfolio (Chapter 6). Most Learning Launches that we have worked on cost under $40,000 and take three months or less, if the team is fully dedicated to doing the assessment.

The precise point at which a decision must be made about a new idea will vary. Let's assume that you have completed a series of Learning Launches on a growth idea and you found no compelling disconfirming data. Assume, also, that you need funding to move to the stage of determining whether your business can make the product. You now want to make a more-sophisticated prototype to engage potential customers in helping to refine it until you are highly confident that it meets their critical needs. Although this is part of the Learning Launch process, you may or may not be ready to do a formal business plan. It depends on the amount of the investment needed to build the prototype and whether or not you have enough evidence for generating sound financial numbers. There are no hard and fast rules here. The team will make its recommendations, but whether and how to go forward with the idea is a judgment call for a management review committee.

A review committee's role is to assess the quantity and quality of the data, the degree of comfort the team has with its recommendations, how cognitive biases were managed, and the risks of going forward. The team's assessment must produce enough information for the review committee to compare the attractiveness and risks of this growth idea with those of other growth ideas under review. The review committee must make its best judgment, choosing a few ideas from a larger group.

The review committee's assessment of the relative strengths of competing ideas and options for continuing their development will be influenced by the kind of Growth Portfolio the company is building and its objectives. We will discuss this in Chapter 6.

6

Creating and Managing a Growth Portfolio

Creating and managing a portfolio of growth initiatives is the final process in the quest for growth and new revenue streams. Previously we discussed how growth requires the right individual and organizational mindsets, an aligned, enabling, and promoting internal System, and processes to identify and test new growth ideas.

In Chapter 1 we talked about creating a pipeline of growth experiments. That is a key concept: identifying potential growth initiatives for your business requires considering many ideas, systematically eliminating the weaker candidates, and continuing to research the better ones through growth experiments (Learning Launches). These will then funnel down further to a workable number of initiatives that will constitute your Growth Portfolio. After the Learning Launch process has identified several good candidates for further development, it is unlikely that your business will want to pursue all of them. Instead, you will want to look at all candidates with an eye to how they, collectively, maximize both short-term and long-term opportunities while minimizing risks. Designing your Growth Portfolio should be a strategic exercise integrated with the overall business strategy processes discussed in Chapter 4.

Strategic Themes

In this chapter we will focus on the design and management of the Growth Portfolio. In designing your Growth Portfolio you will identify your business's short-term and long-term growth needs and categorize them by type of growth. Even before you design your Growth Portfolio, your growth needs will influence what ideas are generated, which survive initial testing, and which you choose to develop further.

The design of a Growth Portfolio requires many of the same analysis tools used in developing strategy. To develop strategy you need data, trend analysis, and scenario planning. Market data, customer data, economic trends, competitor analysis, and technology trends help you decide in what markets and in what ways you will compete. These decisions generate strategic themes that determine the scope or boundaries of your growth ideation, identification, reframing, and experimenting processes. Strategy sets the boundaries of your exploration of Growth Processes. Within those boundaries you have choices about how to grow: improvements, innovations, scaling, acquisitions, or some combination of these. Your strategic choices are influenced by the reality of your current product offerings. Where are they in their life cycle? How long will your current product offerings be strong generators of revenue?

What Is Your Current S-Curves Picture?

In contemplating your growth options, it is important to carefully evaluate your current S-Curves. What do we mean by that? The life cycle of all successful products can be depicted by a classic Sigmoid Curve (S-Curve):

S-Curve

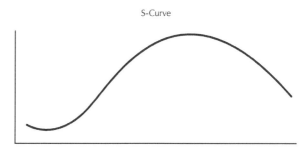

S-Curves begin with a start-up phase and eventually move to a high-growth phase. Growth then peaks and levels off to a product maturity phase before, inevitably, a steady decline. What differs among industries is the speed of that process. Some industries, such as automobiles and steel, have long product life cycles. Others, like consumer electronics and fashion products, are more dynamic and have very short life cycles.

Your current S-Curves determine your Growth Portfolio needs and your choice of Learning Launch experiments. Where do your products fall on the S-Curve? Are your biggest revenue producers headed toward a decline? Do you have other products in the pipeline? Your Growth Portfolio needs influence your choices of Learning Launches as well as your acquisition strategy.

Therefore, you need to create an S-Curve for each current revenue stream with annual estimates of revenue remaining before the inevitable decline.

These annual S-Curve revenue estimates should then be combined into a ten-year projected company revenue stream based on your current portfolio—a mega-S-Curve for your company. That is your baseline—your current strategic reality. It determines the type of growth investments and Learning Launch experiments you should undertake, and it provides a sense of timing—how soon and how much new growth at a minimum you need to pursue in order to avoid a decline in revenues. For example, if your current combined S-Curve positions produced an S-Curve as in the top curve in the figure below, your growth needs are very different from those of a company with an S-Curve profile shown in the middle or bottom curves:

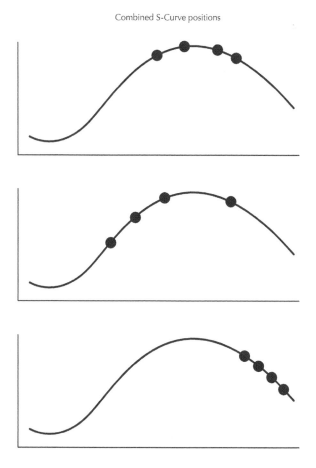

Combined S-Curve positions

Your new growth strategy should be reflected in your Growth Portfolio.

Designing a Growth Portfolio

Within your strategic themes, you still have choices about the types of growth initiative that you undertake. Do you focus primarily on improvement initiatives—getting better, faster, or cheaper? Do you focus on innovating new products or business models? Do you undertake an aggressive acquisition strategy to fill an innovation pipeline void? The answers to those questions depend on the velocity of change in your industry and the S-Curve positions of your existing revenue streams.

Growth initiatives vary on many dimensions. Some produce results quickly; others, slowly. They vary in the likelihood of commercial success as well as the degree of financial risk. Growth initiatives may leverage existing capabilities or require building or buying new ones. All these variables factor into creating a customized Growth Portfolio designed to maximize the probability of producing the growth needed to replace declining S-Curves and to maintain your competitive viability.

The 2 X 2

Our Executive Education participants and consulting clients find it helpful to think about growth along three parameters: classification, timing, and types of growth. Each is important.

First, all growth can be classified as either top line (revenue) or bottom line. Top-line revenue results from selling more goods and services to more customers. Bottom-line growth results from cost savings, efficiencies, or productivity increases.

Second, growth results can be realized quickly or not. Many companies using a Growth Portfolio define "quickly" as two to three years or less. Obviously, long-term growth results are those that take more than two to three years.

Every growth initiative, then, can be classified as impacting either the top line (TL) or bottom line (BL) and doing so either in the short term (ST) or the long term (LT). These classifications are the basis for our standard 2 X 2 diagram:

We will discuss the types of growth in the next section.

The Four Ways to Grow: 2 X 2 X 4

Considering the types of growth is the next piece of the growth puzzle. You have choices in how to invest your growth dollars. There are four primary ways to grow a business: improvements, scaling, innovations, and acquisitions.

Improvements

Improvements are doing what you do, faster, better, or cheaper. Improvements can be to products, business processes, or your business model. In market-leading companies, improvements can produce hundreds of basis points of net profit a year. Often improvements are technology driven. Technology can drive efficiencies and productivity in every functional area of a business, especially in the supply, production, and distribution chains. Technology, likewise, drives information management, customer relationship management and measurement, and the speed of executive decision making.

In our research, we asked many consistent market-leading companies in different industries to describe their core competency. We were surprised when almost all answered "technology." Companies like Sysco, UPS, Best Buy, Paccar, Walmart, Walgreens, and American Eagle Outfitters rely on technology as a growth generator.

Remember the discussion of UPS and Sysco in Chapter 3? UPS has a relentless improvement culture that results in annual increases in bottom-line efficiencies and productivity. Sysco sets an annual growth goal based on improved efficiencies and productivity. The company's current Growth Portfolio includes increasing productivity in its warehouses, national merchandising operations, and supply chain. Sysco also is using technology to revamp its delivery system and build a new customer relationship management system and new management decision tools for its executives, all in the pursuit of growth. Improvements should be the foundation of every company's Growth Portfolio.

Scaling

The second common way to grow is by scaling. Simply put, scaling is doing more of what you are already doing. The result is selling more existing products to more customers. Common scaling growth initiatives include geographical expansions and adding new customer segments. Scaling is the primary way to enter the high-growth phase of an S-Curve.

If you want new S-Curves, then you want to build or buy products and services that can be scaled through your existing customer base. Alternatively, you can purchase a customer segment and scale your offerings through it. Scaling requires more customers and the sale of more products.

Best Buy's growth, historically, has been propelled by geographic expansion and adding new products to scale through the company's existing customer base. Additionally, Best Buy has made strategic acquisitions of new customer segments and a service business in the pursuit of more scaling opportunities. It is constantly adapting to shortening product life cycles and looking for the next product to scale. In addition, it is expanding its channels of distribution far beyond its big-box stores. Best Buy's scaling strategy is currently focused on scaling appliances (in China), gaming software, and tablets, and on new formats that will scale, including Best Buy mobile stores, Best Buy Kiosks, and a new community store format.

Scaling and acquisitions are related: if you cannot create new products to scale or build them fast enough, then you must purchase new products that have been developed and commercialized to some extent by someone else. Stryker Corporation has used this growth strategy for years.[1] According to CFO Curt Hartman, "We have [had] a long history of doing product-line divisional tuck-ins and we tend[ed] to do those under the radar screen. We [went] out and [found] wonderful innovative products that [were] probably under distributed, under marketed, and perhaps need[ed] some manufacturing assistance. We [have had] a great history of doing that."[2]

Innovation

The third way to grow is by innovation. Innovation is a buzzword in the business world today. Every company strives to be innovative. But innovation means different things to different companies. Innovation occurs along a continuum, from small incremental innovation all the way to major disruptive innovation. In many cases there is no difference between an improvement and an incremental innovation. Both can be small changes to existing products or business processes.

For our purposes, however, we distinguish innovations from improvements by defining innovation as doing something new that you have not done before that is a material change. Improvements are close to your core business. Innovation is far away from it. Innovations are big "news" or big "differents." An example of a business model innovation discussed in Chapter 3 was Best Buy's adoption of the customer-centricity model. That was a big change for Best Buy because it required major changes to culture, structure, leadership model, selling processes, measurements, and rewards. For Best Buy, the model was innovative even though it was not unique. In fact, it was almost identical to the business model Bernie Marcus and Arthur Blank used to build Home Depot.

CEOs often look shocked when we state that unless you are cannibalizing (destroying) your own products or distribution channels you are not being innovative. One CEO we work with believes his company is very innovative even though most of his innovation initiatives are cost-reduction efforts. Innovation is in the eye of the beholder.

Acquisitions

The fourth way to grow is through acquisitions. Companies can acquire geography, customers, products, services, or capabilities. Many companies make small strategic acquisitions of new products, new capabilities, or new customer segments that can be scaled. When UPS decided to change its business model to Synchronized Commerce, it made more than 30 acquisitions of capabilities needed to deliver complete logistics solutions. Best Buy acquired the Geek Squad to enter the service business and Magnolia Hi-Fi to enter the home entertainment customer segment. Over the years, Sysco has made more than 120 acquisitions, buying geographical expansion and new products to scale. Coca-Cola's recent growth strategy has been to acquire new products to scale through its distribution system.

Improvements, innovations, and scaling initiatives can be identified, developed, and commercialized through the Growth Processes discussed in the previous chapters. Acquisitions require different processes and capabilities, including due diligence and merger integration.

The "Panic" Acquisition

Unfortunately, too many companies wake up to their S-Curve challenges only after their existing S-Curves have peaked. In many cases, because they have failed to keep growth investments in the pipeline, they are forced to seed new growth quickly. This is a challenge: over time, improvements may produce meaningful small growth numbers but do not usually generate new S-Curves. Genuine innovations are high risk and take time to develop and commercialize. Scaling will not be a viable option for re-energizing your S-Curve without something new to scale. Another common alternative to keeping your business growing is to leverage your capabilities into another industry segment. But, again, that takes years.

As a result, companies often feel compelled to do a big acquisition. The bigger the company, the bigger the acquisition must be to revitalize the S-Curve. However, large acquisitions come with large financial and merger integration risks.

We think there is a better way to address the inevitable declines in S-Curves. That is to proactively and strategically create and manage a growth pipeline of ideas. Consistently fostering idea generation and experimentation and developing a Growth Portfolio attuned to the short- and long-term needs of your business will make "panic" acquisitions unnecessary.

Before we move on to designing your Growth Portfolio, one other research finding has proven to be useful in thinking about alternative ways to grow.

Common Growth Progressions

One of our research projects, in addition to research conducted by McKinsey & Company,[3] found that most companies grow in the same progression.[4] We have combined these findings to produce the following growth checklist, which can be used in considering the range of ways businesses grow:

1. Geographical expansion
2. Introduction of complementary products to existing customers
3. Expand to new customer segments with existing products
4. Add complementary services for existing customers
5. Focus on cost efficiencies
6. Focus on technological productivity in the supply chain, logistics, and manufacturing functions
7. Add or acquire (usually on a small scale) strategic new products, customer segments, or services
8. Move from product-centricity to selling solutions
9. Start over at step one and simultaneously improve in all areas

This checklist is a good tool to be used to generate growth ideas.

Designing Your Growth Portfolio

As discussed earlier in this chapter, growth initiatives can be classified by several variables. In our 2 X 2 matrix, we classify growth initiatives according to whether they will affect the top or bottom line and whether they will do so in the short term or long term (see the 2 X 2 diagram above).

To use this matrix in designing your Growth Portfolio, you first will need to place each current growth initiative in the appropriate quadrant. Note that we do not mean your existing product portfolio. Rather, growth initiatives are your new growth activities that are works-in-process. We suggest using the following categories to plot your positions. You will also need an easy way to label the type of growth initiative:

Types of Initiatives

Improvement Labels	
IP = Improvement to existing product	IBP = Improvement to business process
IT = Improvement to technology	

Innovation Labels	
NP = New product	NBP = New business process
NBM = New business model	NI = Industry diversification
NC = New capabilities	NT = New technology platform

Scaling Labels	
SG = Geographical expansion	SS = Scaling new customer segment
SP = Scaling existing product	SBP = Scaling business process

Acquisition Labels	
AG = Acquire geography	AP = Acquire new products
AC = Acquire capabilities	AS = Acquire new customer segment

We need to add one more dimension in classifying the initiatives in your Growth Portfolio: *risk*. Determining the risk of a growth initiative requires a judgment about the probability of success and how much financial risk you are undertaking relative to your broad financial capabilities. It also requires a judgment about the size of the particular investment relative to the total amount of growth investment dollars you have available. Remember that you need to generate many growth ideas to produce a small number of growth experiments—Learning Launches. These produce an even smaller number of initiatives that roll into a Growth Portfolio. Building a Growth Portfolio is similar to building an investment portfolio. Good investors diversify and hedge their risks.

The degree of financial risk associated with a growth initiative will be a function of your size and circumstances. One million dollars may be a small risk to a large company but a "bet the ranch" risk to a small company. Financial risks are independent of the probability of success. The question you must answer is, "How much will it hurt my business if the amount invested in this initiative is lost?"

The second aspect of risk is the risk of failure—or the probability of success. This informs your decisions regarding how you populate your Growth Portfolio. So assessing the risks of a growth initiative is really two assessments: a financial downside assessment and a probability of success assessment.

The easiest way to create a concrete picture of risks is to color code growth initiatives according to a range of characteristics. Green denotes a high probability of success *and* low financial risk. Yellow denotes a medium probability of success *and* medium financial risk. Red denotes a low probability of success *or* high financial risk.

Your 2 X 2 X 4 X 3 Growth Portfolio

Once you have assigned the above labels and colors to your growth initiatives, you should create an even more detailed, 2 X 2 X 4 X 3 grid of your current Growth Portfolio. This picture shows the character of your investments (top or bottom line), the expected timing of major returns (short or long term), the types of investments (improvements, scaling, innovation, or acquisitions), and the risk profile (green, yellow, or red).

From your current S-Curves picture, you have a projection of your future growth needs. Some of your current products will continue to produce for some time, while others will decline. Your goal is to fill the pipeline with new growth initiatives to keep the collective S-Curve of your business portfolio in the growth mode. Your specific growth needs will also determine your choice of ideas to put through the Learning Launch experimentation process.

Armed with the information you generated by labeling and color coding your initiatives, you can determine your gaps and begin to create a diversified portfolio of initiatives designed to both fill existing gaps and generate new S-Curves. The goal should be to build a pipeline of new potential S-Curves, keeping in mind that not all of your initiatives will meet your expectations.

Let's look at a recent example of a successful company, Starbucks Corporation, which needed to create a new Growth Portfolio to compensate for some bad decisions. This story demonstrates the dynamic creation of a diverse portfolio, the need to create new scaling opportunities, and the use of Learning Launches to test innovative initiatives.

Starbucks's New Growth Portfolio[5]

Founded in 1971, Starbucks was for over 30 years a high-growth company fueled by geographical expansion, new store openings in current markets, and new products. By the end of 2007, Starbucks owned over 8,500 U.S. stores, operated or licensed over 4,300 international stores, and was generating nearly $8 billion of revenue. From 2000 to 2007, it had accelerated new-store openings and made many operational changes that damaged both customer experience and employee engagement. This growth resulted in underperforming new stores, the cannibalization of existing stores, a nine-fold increase in liabilities, a nearly five-fold increase in non-cancellable operating leases, a substantial decline in same-store sales increases, and a substantial loss in market value.

Starbucks suffered serious self-inflicted wounds from this overexpansion. After aggressively pursuing growth as a public company for almost 20 years, it hit a major speed bump, to say the least, which was exacerbated by the domestic economic crisis. This significant downturn required that Chairman Howard Schultz return as CEO in January 2008 to get Starbucks back on track.

Starbucks's prior success stemmed from its ability to scale a store concept, creating world-class processes and replicating them in its stores across the United States and abroad. It had set its sights and bet its name on capturing market share in every category open for competition. Its rapid growth and successes, however, hastened its downfall as the luster of its brand faded. Yet, despite grim pronouncements from analysts, the company was far from dead, and Schultz was determined to resuscitate it. He thought he could accomplish this by reigniting the company's growth in a U.S. market already saturated with Starbucks locations.

The company announced two rounds of store closures totaling approximately 900 stores and affecting more than 18,000 jobs. A disproportionate number of the stores that were closed had been built after 2006, at a time when growth goals forced the company to compromise its standards, including real estate site selection. The company also oversaturated many first-tier markets and built too many stores in second-tier markets.

How to Reignite Growth?

Schultz considered his options for future growth: improvements, innovations, scaling, and strategic acquisitions. Absent a major acquisition, he knew, the most viable opportunity for high growth was through scaling. But he wondered whether growth should continue to be the goal or whether to focus instead on improvements—getting better rather than bigger.

Improvements

In 2008 and 2009, it became increasingly difficult for Starbucks to improve top-line results, so it announced it would focus on the bottom line—"fine-tuning labor, implementing programs, and rolling out software to target operational efficiencies." In this context Schultz stated:

> For 10 years, we have been focusing our resources on ever-increasing growth. The growth has been quite staggering, the number of new customers has been quite incredible, and that has been where our resources have been applied. We're now in a situation with this pause, one could say, so that we really get an opportunity for the first time to go back and look at how we do our work, how we're set up, and importantly, how we can optimize the returns from individual stores.[6]

Management Tools

As a key part of its improvement strategy, Starbucks redirected the duties of managers. District managers, whose jobs had been focused on expansion, now primarily supported store operations. Focusing less on expansion meant that each district manager would eventually be responsible for 12 stores instead of eight. Store managers, who had changed stores often to support expansion, now stayed in one place and focused on improvements. By working with the same crew of employees, managers improved relationships with the team in a store, benefiting the customers who entered it.

To support the development of store managers, the company offered new training courses on business acumen. A new dashboard software was implemented to provide simple, easy-to-understand store operation metrics to store managers and the district managers who supported them.

Rationalize Supply Chain

Starbucks had been working with 40 different bakeries to produce a variety of recipes with little differentiation. For example, there were 11 different banana-bread recipes in the system and multiple variations of blueberry muffins. By stocking in its stores only the best products in each class, Starbucks reduced the number of SKUs. The company then implemented a simplified and more-intuitive POS (point of sale) system.

New Processes

Starbucks continued to focus on operational efficiencies to improve the company's bottom line. CFO Troy Alstead noted that for fiscal year 2008 store labor cost the company $2.5 billion. More importantly, the percentage of revenue needed to cover store labor had increased steadily over the preceding decade. Although this was partially the result of offering items that were more complicated to prepare, such as Frappuccinos, there was room for improvement. The previous decade had introduced a variety of new drink recipes—some on a seasonal basis and some that became long-term offerings. However, the focus of barista training for these beverages had been on the recipe rather than on the routine. The company now focused on creating repeatable drink-preparation routines for baristas to follow.

As Starbucks studied processes within its stores, it noticed one particular area for improvement: cost of quality. "Cost of quality" is Starbucks-speak for product waste—that which is not sold and must be discarded. Examples included excess steamed milk that could not be used, prepared food that was not consumed, and brewed coffee that had exceeded its hold time. Starbucks identified several simple cost-saving opportunities it had not previously pursued because of its rapid pace of growth. By altering some practices and procedures, the company was able to cut cost-of-quality expenses by $400 million in 2009 and $200 million in the first part of 2010. Furthermore, these cost efficiencies were sustainable and did not harm the customer experience.

A Business Process Innovation—The Learning Launch

Recognizing the tremendous savings that came from its foray into stemming the cost of quality, Starbucks took cost savings and process implementation in a new direction and began to develop a "lean" store. As unveiled at the 2008 Biennial Analyst Conference, a lean store was a test store that adopted continuous improvement practices by:

- Reducing motions behind the bar
- Allowing three baristas to stay in fixed positions while a fourth person was responsible for supporting the rest of the activities
- Simplifying partner training
- Lowering labor costs
- Increasing customer satisfaction and speed of service

The first lean store debuted in 2009, adding to the cost savings that helped Starbucks during the economic downturn. The company understood, however, that it could not grow only through cost savings but must also continue to innovate.

New Products

Although Starbucks's presence in the handcrafted beverages market was strong, the company recognized that its market share could be dramatically increased in segments such as food, brewed coffee, teas, and instant coffee. It launched a variety of initiatives to capture those segments of the market.

Coffee

With only 14 percent market share in the brewed-coffee category, Starbucks was underrepresented. The company had loyal customers flocking to its stores for their favorite espresso drinks every day, but the same was not true for its brewed coffee. Brewed coffee had a lower price point than espresso drinks and was less labor-intensive to serve to customers. After carefully developing a signature taste, Starbucks introduced "Pike Place Roast," a "consistent, everyday coffee that [customers] could count on."[7] Named after Seattle's iconic Pike Place Market, the new coffee performed exceptionally well, particularly on the East Coast, and gave Starbucks another opportunity to tell the "Starbucks Story." Along with this new roast, the company established practices to ensure that its taste was always fresh by bringing back in-store grinding and reducing the brewed-coffee hold time from 60 to 30 minutes.

To further ensure the success of the Pike Place Roast, Starbucks distributed seven million promotional cards. The card was made of coated paper rather than plastic and offered a "free cup of Pike Place Roast every Wednesday, for eight Wednesdays."[8] Unlike coupons, which generally had 2 to 3 percent redemption, this card and the similar cards that followed had 15 to 20 percent redemption. After eight weeks of Pike Place Roast, some customers were well on their way to developing a habit.

Instant Coffee

Starbucks considered offering instant coffee, a $23 billion global category that had not seen any real innovation in more than 50 years. This was not a new idea for the company. Almost 20 years earlier, a young man named Don Valencia had appeared in the Pike Place Market store claiming that he had "cracked the code" on brewing instant Starbucks coffee. The store manager was so impressed with the taste of Valencia's special instant brew that just two days later he sent him to Howard Schultz's office. As a result, Valencia agreed to move his family from Sacramento to Seattle and became the company's first head of R&D.

Although Valencia and his team were responsible for the formulation of the wildly successful Starbucks bottled Frappuccino drink, he wasn't able to bring the instant coffee to market in the scale necessary without compromising its quality. When Schultz returned as CEO, he asked the R&D team to use Valencia's new technologies to take a fresh look at creating a scalable instant coffee worthy of the Starbucks name. Unfortunately, Valencia died of cancer two years before Starbucks was able to bring his original invention to fruition: a product called VIA, loosely named after him.

The new coffee, known as "ready brew" rather than "instant," sold for less than $1 per cup and was packaged in single servings for easy, on-the-go preparation. Using 100 percent Arabica beans, rather than industry standard Robusta beans, it was not hard for Starbucks to improve on taste. Plus, the single serving, go-anywhere package was a hit with customers. Because of the company's extensive retail network, VIA had almost 30,000 instant distribution points. Just in time for ready brew's first summer on the market, Starbucks introduced VIA

Ready Brew Iced Coffee. By the time VIA products had been on the market for ten months, they had reached $100 million in sales, a level that the bottled Frappuccino took three years to reach.

In August 2010, Starbucks introduced a new line of exclusive coffees called Starbucks Reserve.[9] These "ultra-premium, single-origin" coffees aimed at the higher echelon of coffee drinkers—Starbucks's original audience. In a preview sale on Gilt.com, an exclusive, members-only website featuring designer and luxury items, Starbucks Reserve's first offering, Galápagos San Cristobel, sold out in 12 hours.

Teas

Although Starbucks had a 30 percent market share in the "coffee away from home" category, its share of the comparable tea category was only 5 percent. The company had experienced success in this market with chai and shaken teas, but there was still room to grow. In 2008, to supplement the $1 billion Tazo Tea line, the company introduced "handcrafted full-leaf teas." The new tea concoctions were promoted for their great taste and health benefits.[10]

Food

Schultz had denounced the company's food offerings in one highly publicized memo, charging that the smell of the food, by masking the smell of coffee, took away from the "romance" of the store. The fact remained that there was room to grow in the food category as some customers made two stops in the morning: one for breakfast and one for coffee. In 2008, food sales made up 17 percent of retail store revenue.

Research indicated that customers craved healthy breakfast alternatives, so Starbucks introduced oatmeal: a healthy breakfast whose smell would not interfere with store ambiance. The company then decided to delve into the $2 billion smoothie market with a product line called Vivanno. With 80 percent of its customers reportedly consuming smoothies and only a couple of key players in a market captured mostly by mom-and-pop shops, Starbucks saw a market opportunity.

In February 2009, the company introduced a value-meal program, which it referred to as a food-and-drink-pairing program. The move was prompted by three major factors: increased competition from the fast-food sector, the recession, and changes in consumer habits.[11] Meanwhile, Starbucks, faced with rivals whose advertising highlighted the price of its drinks, attempted to dispel the "myth" of the $4 cup of coffee.

Learning Launches of New Store Concepts

From its inception, Starbucks experimented with new store concepts, hoping to create one as successful as the original. In July 2009, it opened the first of what would be three "un-Starbucks" stores created by its design guru Arthur Rubinfeld. These remodeled stores dropped the Starbucks name, logo, and other branding in favor of neighborhood names such as "15th Avenue Coffee and Tea," "Roy Street Coffee and Tea," and "Olive Way." The only hint that these new locations were affiliated with Starbucks was the small "Inspired by Starbucks" notice on their front doors.

The new stores, with their rustic design, evoked a neighborhood coffeeshop feeling, rather than that of a corporate giant. One reviewer noted, "In the spirit of a traditional coffeehouse, it [served] wine and beer, [hosted] live music and poetry readings, and [sold] espresso from a manual machine rather than the automated type found in most Starbucks stores."[12] Rubinfeld's move was approved by Morningstar analyst R.J. Hottovy: "I think the idea of trying to localize the business, that's an aspect that will certainly work and help differentiate the brand and make it a lot less cookie-cutter than what you see in standard Starbucks."[13]

The Olive Way store, which opened about a year after 15th Avenue Coffee and Tea and Roy Street Coffee and Tea, was a grander experiment. At 2,500 square feet, it was furnished for comfort with cushy chairs and an indoor-outdoor fireplace. It featured a "coffee theater" and "a menu with wine from the Pacific Northwest's vineyards and beer from local craft brewers."[14] In addition, Olive Way's menu offered savory foods to pair with the coffee, wine, and beer on the menu.

Scaling: Franchising Seattle's Best Coffee

For Starbucks, a major source of tension existed between company-operated and licensed stores. The leadership knew that allowing stores to be run by any entity other than the company itself would cause a deviation from the Starbucks Experience. As a result, the company licensed stores only when it was absolutely impossible to install a company-operated store to serve a specific market. In 2005, when Walmart aggressively pursued the idea of placing a Starbucks inside its stores, Starbucks CEO Jim Donald had responded, "We'd love to be in Walmart parking lots with company-operated stores."[15]

After Schultz was re-installed as CEO, one growth suggestion was for the company to offer franchise opportunities and shutter company-owned stores. Schultz disagreed:

That would have given us a war chest of cash and significantly increased return on capital. It's a good argument economically. It's a good argument for shareholder value. But it would have fractured the culture of the company. You can't get out of this by trying to navigate with a different road map, one that isn't true to yourself. You have to be authentic, you have to be true, and you have to believe in your heart that this is going to work.[16]

Although the Starbucks name would not be associated with franchising, the company did not ignore the obvious market opportunity. Seattle's Best, a sub-brand of Starbucks long overshadowed by the main brand, announced in 2010 that it would offer franchise opportunities. Almost immediately, it had a "deep pipeline of franchisees," and the opportunity was named one of the top ten franchising concepts.[17] Around that time, further development of the Seattle's Best brand was under way: Subway and Burger King restaurants already served the coffee in their stores, and packaged-coffee sales in retail outlets came next. By the fall of 2010, Seattle's Best coffee had reached its goal of being served in 30,000 places, a ten-fold increase since March of the same year.[18]

International Scaling Opportunities

In 2010, Starbucks had 5,500 stores outside the United States, spanning 51 countries, and projected more growth, particularly in China, Brazil, India, and Russia. Those countries were promising markets because of their affinity for the Starbucks Experience and the corresponding growth of their upper and middle classes.[19]

Another international scaling opportunity existed in the food-service business segment—brewed coffee in hotels and restaurants—which had been developed only in Canada, leaving the rest of the world ripe for expansion. The company also anticipated that its VIA would sell well globally, particularly in Japan and the United Kingdom, where 70 to 80 percent of the coffee consumed was instant. Starbucks launched other ready-to-drink products in China and Korea.

Growth Initiatives Do Fail

Not all of Schultz's initiatives were successful. The Starbucks version of a value meal, the pairing program, quietly fizzled. Despite his assertion that warmed breakfast sandwiches would be eliminated from all North American stores by the end of fiscal year 2008, they were not. Only half of the tea concoctions took hold, and the rest were removed from the menu. But Schultz, known for rolling with the punches and focusing more on wins than losses, kept his cool and continued innovating. For each initiative that failed, there was at least one that kept the company moving forward.

Lessons from Starbucks

Starbucks created a diversified portfolio of growth initiatives: improvements, innovations, and scaling. Improvements were short term and low risk. Scaling was both short and long term, and low to medium risk. Innovations were tested through Learning Launches with low financial risks because the investment was an allowable loss—a small bet: one new "lean" store and three different new concept stores.

Starbucks experimented and accepted failures. The company also cut its losses quickly. Almost every growth initiative had as its ultimate goal scaling: either scaling new process improvements or new products through existing stores. Franchising and international expansion were also scaling initiatives.

The Starbucks story evolves, but at this point its Growth Portfolio has produced impressive results.

The Starbucks example, plus the classification tools discussed above, should guide you in creating your Growth Portfolio. Creating a Growth Portfolio, however, is only the first step. Actively managing that portfolio is the next step.

Managing a Growth Portfolio

Managing a Growth Portfolio, like managing a Learning Launch, as discussed in Chapter 5, is part science and part art. The science part is having real-time high-quality data and managing the risks of cognitive biases. The art part comes down to good judgment. For our purposes, we will raise a few common Growth Portfolio management questions.

Centralize or Decentralize Management of the Growth Portfolio?

Whether to centralize or decentralize the management of the Growth Portfolio depends on who controls (or should control) its composition—corporate or individual business units, or a hybrid model.

We have seen two common answers to this question—both hybrids. First, some companies delegate control of improvements and mature scaling initiatives to business units while centralizing innovation, new scaling initiatives, and acquisitions. Other companies delegate all growth initiatives to business units but keep corporate control of all capital investments above a set amount per business unit—an approach that effectively centralizes control of major acquisitions and technology investments.

Timing of Portfolio Reviews?

How often should you review your Growth Portfolio? It depends. We generally recommend quarterly reviews, but in certain situations more frequent reviews are advisable, such as when a business is facing a competitive or financial crisis. We call those "911" reviews.

The primary purpose of normal reviews is evaluating data to determine whether certain growth initiatives should be killed and investment dollars reallocated to other existing or new investments. Maintaining the balance in the Growth Portfolio between short-term and long-term needs is also critical.

Minimum Innovation Investments?

We are often asked what the minimum percentage of investment dollars is that should be allocated to innovation—truly new initiatives. Again, it depends. We know from experience that in a business environment dominated by making quarterly earnings numbers, operating units will push to allocate all investments to opportunities that will help meet those short-term goals. This tends to drive a focus on improvements and incremental, close-to-the-core innovation. This focus is especially the case if business unit leaders are measured and rewarded primarily on short-term results. This short-term focus may address quarterly earnings but probably prevents many good growth opportunities from even being considered.

As you would imagine, there is no magic number for the amount a business should devote to innovation investments. It will depend on your industry, your existing S-Curves, your innovation capabilities, and your priorities. Some companies set goals of the percentage of revenue to be derived from new products by a certain date in the near future. Others reserve a percentage of investment dollars for innovation and make those investments at the corporate level, not the business unit level. Still others—mainly large companies—conclude that their size makes innovation unlikely and decide to achieve innovation by acquisitions.

What we do know is that whether you build or buy innovation, you need dedicated resources allocated to the type of innovation that, if done by competitors, would cause material harm to your existing business. In many cases such threatening innovation is technology-based. Today technology innovation that could harm a business is emerging not only in the usual high-technology areas but also from neuroscience, complexity theory, and behavioral sciences.

Percentage of Business Unit Leadership Compensation
to Be Determined by Business Unit Results?

How to compensate business unit leadership for growth initiatives is a frequent question. The answer depends on the kind of behavior you want to drive. Do you want people motivated to collaborate and act as stewards of the enterprise, or do you want each business unit to operate more like a stand-alone company? Is corporate an enterprise or a holding company?

This is the same kind of structure question we addressed in Chapter 3. The answer to what you centralize and how you give autonomy to business units is bigger than a control issue. It plays a material role in either enabling or inhibiting the entrepreneurial behaviors necessary for exploration and innovation.

Velocity of Growth Portfolio Change?

The speed at which your Growth Portfolio evolves will (or should) depend on your industry, its composition, and the rigor of your reviews. Best Buy, for example, is in a high-velocity industry influenced by ever-changing technology and product development. The company has publicly disclosed its Growth Portfolio for over five years, during which the portfolio has experienced major shifts. Best Buy has materially changed its international expansion strategy and its China strategy. It conducted Learning Launches of totally different concept stores, none of which has advanced. It has looked at the financing business. It has expanded its private branded products and evolved the Geek Squad beyond computer services.

Likewise, Sysco announced a few years ago that its new growth area would be in providing logistics and distribution service to other food suppliers. This initiative has not advanced. Instead, Sysco continues to build out its strategy of internal regional redistribution centers.

A Growth Portfolio should be diversified, and it should balance short-term and long-term needs. If you are experimenting, you will try new things and many will fail. Many companies are able to decide quickly to kill or table initiatives that do not look promising. Then they replenish the Growth Portfolio with new experiments. Other companies in industries based on scientific research, such as pharmaceuticals, take years making the determination to go forward or shelve an idea. In both cases, companies are playing probability games, placing many small bets and remaining wary of placing a large bet too early.

Reference Matter

Appendix

Tools and Templates, by Chapter

Notes

Chapter 1

Portions of this chapter are adapted from Edward D. Hess, "Growth is a Dynamic Confluence of Strategy, Entrepreneurship, and Values," UVA-S-0196 (Charlottesville, VA: Darden Business Publishing, 2011) with permission of the University of Virginia Darden School Foundation.

1. All anonymous manager quotes in this chapter originally appeared in Jeanne Liedtka, "Growth Leaders Research Project," Batten Institute, Darden School of Business, Charlottesville, 2005–2006.

2. John Henry Clippinger III, ed., *The Biology of Business: Decoding the Natural Laws of Enterprise* (San Francisco: Jossey-Bass, 1999), 7.

3. Melanie Mitchell, *Complexity: A Guided Tour* (New York: Oxford University Press, 2009), 182–183.

4. Edward D. Hess, *The Road to Organic Growth: How Great Companies Consistently Grow Marketshare From Within* (New York: McGraw-Hill, 2007).

5. Gary Hamel, "Innovation's New Math," *Fortune*, July 9, 2001.

Chapter 2

1. All named and anonymous manager quotes in this chapter originally appeared in Jeanne Liedtka, "Growth Leaders Research Project," Batten Institute, Darden School of Business, Charlottesville, 2005–2006. See also Jeanne Liedtka, Sean Carr and Andrew King, "Leading Organic Growth: Module Caselets," UVA-BP-0541 (Charlottesville, VA: Darden Business Publishing, 2009). This research also was featured in Jeanne Liedtka, Robert Rosen, and Robert Wiltbank, *The Catalyst: How You Can Become an Extraordinary Growth Leader* (New York: Crown Business, 2009).

2. For a further discussion of the concept of mindsets, see Carol S. Dweck, *Mindset: The New Psychology of Success* (New York: Random House, 2006).

3. E. Tory Higgins, "Beyond Pleasure and Pain," *American Psychologist* 52 (1997).

Chapter 3

This chapter is adapted from Edward D. Hess, "Growth is Much More than Just a Strategy: It's a System," UVA-S-0197 (Charlottesville, VA: Darden Business Publishing, 2011) with permission of the University of Virginia Darden School Foundation. All figures and tables included in this chapter other than "Internal Growth System" originally appeared therein.

1. Edward D. Hess and Robert K. Kazanjian, eds., *The Search for Organic Growth* (Cambridge: Cambridge University Press, 2006), 147–48 and 103–123; Mark Lipton, *Guiding Growth: How Vision Keeps Companies on Course* (Boston: Harvard Business School Press, 2003), 36–37; Mathew S. Olson and Derek van Bever, *Stall Points: Most Companies Stop Growing—Yours Doesn't Have To* (New Haven, CT: Yale University Press, 2008); Sven Smit, Caroline M. Thompson, and S. Patrick Viguerie, "The Do-or-Die Struggle for Growth," *McKinsey Quarterly* 3 (2005), 35–45; Robert R. Wiggins and Timothy W. Rueffi, "Sustained Competitive Advantage: Temporal Dynamics and the Incidence of Persistence of Superior Economic Performance," *Organization Science* 13, no. 1 (2002), 100; "Schumpeter's Ghost: Is Hypercompetition Making the Best of Times Shorter?" *Strategic Management Journal* 26, no. 10 (2005), 887–911.

2. Edward D. Hess, *The Road to Organic Growth: How Great Companies Consistently Grow Marketshare From Within* (New York: McGraw-Hill, 2007).

3. Tom Cross and Alexander B. Horniman, "Dow Chemical Polyolefins and Elastomers R&D: Sustaining High Performance," Case Study UVA-OB-O813 (Charlottesville, VA: Darden Business Publishing, 2003).

4. Edward D. Hess, "Sysco Corporation," Case Study UVA-S-0140 (Charlottesville, VA: Darden Business Publishing, 2007). (This case has been updated for material events.); Edward D. Hess, "United Parcel Service of America, Inc.," Case Study UVA-S-0143 (Charlottesville, VA: Darden Business Publishing, 2007). (This case has been updated for material events.)

5. Edward D. Hess, "Tiffany & Company," Case Study UVA-S-0141 (Charlottesville, VA: Darden Business Publishing, 2007). (This case has been updated for material events.)

6. Edward D. Hess, "Room & Board," Case Study UVA-S-0150 (Charlottesville, VA: Darden Business Publishing, 2008).

7. For the TSYS story, see Hess, *The Road to Organic Growth*, 129–37; Edward D. Hess and Cassy Eriksson, "Starbucks Corporation (A)," Case Study UVA-S-0175 (Charlottesville, VA: Darden Business Publishing, 2010); Edward D. Hess and Cassy Eriksson, "Starbucks Corporation (B)," Case Study UVA-S-0176 (Charlottesville, VA: Darden Business Publishing, 2010); Edward D. Hess and Shizuka Modica, "Levy Restaurants," Case Study UVA-S-0155 (Charlottesville, VA: Darden Business Publishing, 2009).

8. Hess, "United Parcel Service of America, Inc." All quotes are directly from the case.

9. Lou Gerstner, *Who Says Elephants Can't Dance? Inside IBM's Historic Turnaround* (New York: Harper Collins, 2002), 182. For more on the IBM story, see Lynda M. Applegate, Robert Austin, and Elizabeth Collins, "IBM's Decade of Transformation: Turnaround to Growth," HBS No. 9-805-130 (Boston: Harvard Business School Publishing, 2005).

10. Edward D. Hess, "Best Buy Co., Inc.," Case Study UVA-S-0142 (Charlottesville, VA: Darden Business Publishing, 2007). (This case has been updated for material events.) All quotes are directly from the case.

11. Hess, "Sysco Corporation." All quotes are directly from the case.

12. Edward D. Hess and Cassy Eriksson, "Stryker Corporation," Case Study UVA-S-0174 (Charlottesville, VA: Darden Business Publishing, 2010).

13. Hess and Modica, "Levy Restaurants."

14. Ibid.

15. Hess, "Sysco Corporation."

16. Hess, "Best Buy Co., Inc."

17. Hess, "Sysco Corporation."

18. Ibid.

19. Hess, *Road to Organic Growth*, 94–95.

20. Hess, "Best Buy Co., Inc."

21. Ibid.

Chapter 4

1. All named and anonymous manager quotes in this chapter originally appeared in Jeanne Liedtka, "Growth Leaders Research Project," Batten Institute, Darden School of Business, Charlottesville, 2005–2006. See also Jeanne Liedtka, Sean Carr, and Andrew King, "Leading Organic Growth: Module Caselets," UVA-BP-0541 (Charlottesville, VA: Darden Business Publishing, 2009).

2. Ibid.

3. Peter Senge, *The Fifth Discipline: The Art & Practice of the Learning Organization* (New York: Doubleday Business, 1994), 198.

4. Steven Johnson, *Where Good Ideas Come From: The Natural History of Innovation* (New York: Riverhead Books, 2010), 42.

5. Johnson, *Where Good Ideas Come From*, 152.

6. Richard J. Boland Jr. and Frank Collopy, "Design Matters for Management," in *Managing as Design*, Boland Jr. and Collopy, eds. (Stanford: Stanford University Press, 2004), chap 1.

7. Stuart Kauffman, *Investigations* (Oxford: Oxford University Press, 2000).

8. Johnson, *Where Good Ideas Come From*, 31.

9. Tom Peters, *The Circle of Innovation: You Can't Shrink Your Way to Greatness* (New York: Knopf, 1997), 326. Quoting George Colony, CEO of Forrester Research.

10. Robert Friedel and Jeanne Liedtka, "Possibility Thinking: Lessons from Breakthrough Engineering," *Journal of Business Strategy*, 28, no. 4 (2007).

11. Johnson, *Where Good Ideas Come From*, 22.

12. Gary Hamel and C.K. Prahalad, *Competing for the Future* (Boston: Harvard University Press, 1994), 129–30.

13. Glen T. Senk, CEO, Urban Outfitters, Inc. (Leadership Speaker Series, University of Virginia Darden School of Business, Charlottesville, VA, February 4, 2009).

14. Marion K. Poetz and Martin Schreier, "The Value of Crowdsourcing: Can Users Really Compete with Professionals in Generating New Product Ideas?" *Journal of Product Innovation Management* 29, no. 2 (2012).

Chapter 5

This chapter is adapted from Edward D. Hess, "Learning Launches: Growth Results from Experimental Learning," UVA-S-0198 (Charlottesville, VA: Darden Business Publishing, 2011) with permission of the University of Virginia Darden School Foundation, which work is an adaptation and extension of Jeanne M. Liedtka and Edward D. Hess, "Designing Learning Launches" UVA-BP-0529 (Charlottesville: Darden Business Publishing, 2009) based on Hess's teaching, research, and consulting experience with Learning Launches since 2008. Other researchers have also documented the need to engage in experimental processes: See Peter Skarzynski and Rowan Gibson, *Innovation to the Core: A Blueprint for Transforming the Way Your Company Innovates* (Boston: Harvard Business Press, 2008) and Alexander B. van Putten and Ian C. MacMillan, *Unlocking Opportunities for Growth: How to Profit from Uncertainty While Limiting Your Risk* (Upper Saddle River, NJ: Wharton School Publishing, 2009).

1. Peter F. Drucker, *Innovation and Entrepreneurship* (New York: HarperCollins, 1985), 243.

Chapter 6

This chapter is adapted from Edward D. Hess, "Creating a Growth Portfolio," UVA-S-0199 (Charlottesville, VA: Darden Business Publishing, 2011) with permission of the University of Virginia Darden School Foundation. All figures and tables included in this chapter originally appeared therein.

1. Edward D. Hess and Cassy Eriksson, "Stryker Corporation," Case Study UVA-S-0174 (Charlottesville, VA: Darden Business Publishing, 2010).

2. Ibid.

3. Mehrdad Baghai, Stephen C. Coley, David White, Charles Conn, and Robert J. McLean, "Staircases to Growth," *McKinsey Quarterly* 4 (1996).

4. Edward D. Hess, *Smart Growth: Building an Enduring Business by Managing the Risks of Growth* (New York: Columbia Business School Publishing, 2010), 79; Edward D. Hess, *The Road to Organic Growth: How Great Companies Consistently Grow Marketshare from Within* (New York: McGraw-Hill, 2007), 64–69.

5. Edward D. Hess and Cassy Eriksson, "Starbucks Corporation (A)," Case Study UVA-S-0175, University of Virginia Darden Foundation, Charlottesville, 2010; Edward D. Hess and Cassy Eriksson, "Starbucks Corporation (B)," Case Study UVA-S-0176, University of Virginia Darden Foundation, Charlottesville, 2010.

6. "Starbucks 2008 Biennial Analyst Conference," *CQ FD Disclosure* (formerly, *Voxant FD Wire*), December 4, 2008, Factiva (FNDW000020081211e4c40005o).

7. Ibid.

8. Ibid.

9. Starbucks, "Starbucks Reserve™ Premium Single-Origin Coffee Line Launches in Select U.S. Markets This Fall," Press Release, August 16, 2010, Starbucks Newsroom, http://news.starbucks.com/article_display.cfm?article_id=426.

10. "Starbucks 2008 Biennial Analyst Conference."

11. Bruce Horovitz, "Struggling Starbucks Unveils Menu Deal to Halt Slide," *USA Today*, February 9, 2009.

12. Melissa Allison, "Starbucks Tests New Names for Stores," *Seattle Times*, July 16, 2009.

13. Ashley M. Heher, "Starbucks 'Coffee Theater': Wine, Beer Among Experiments At 'Olive Way' Testing Store," *Huffington Post*, June 25, 2010, www.huffingtonpost.com/2010/06/25/starbucks-coffee-theater_n_625142.html.

14. Ibid.

15. Patricia Sellers, "Starbucks: The Next Generation," *Fortune*, April 4, 2005.

16. Adi Ignatius, "The HBR Interview: 'We Had to Own the Mistakes,'" *Harvard Business Review* 88, no. 7/8 (2010), 111.

17. "Starbucks Shareholders Meeting—Final," *CQ FD Disclosure*, March 24, 2010, Factiva (FND W000020100407e63o001gt).

18. Starbucks, "Seattle's Best Coffee Reaches Milestone Goal of Establishing 30,000 Places to Enjoy a Cup of Its Coffee," Press Release, September 2, 2010, Starbucks Newsroom, http://news.starbucks .com/article_display.cfm?article_id=435.

19. "Starbucks 2008 Biennial Analyst Conference."

The Authors

Edward D. Hess

As a former investment banker and strategy consultant, Ed began his organic growth research in 2002 at the Goizueta Business School at Emory University and continued his research of high-growth public and private companies upon joining the Darden Graduate School of Business at the University of Virginia in 2007. When he began, he was surprised that organic growth was defined by size metrics or as being the opposite of acquisitive growth and was not widely researched by academics. He first developed the "Organic Growth Index," a financial model designed to illuminate high organic growth companies. That led to his research of the characteristics of 22 such companies, which was published in the book *The Road to Organic Growth: How Great Companies Consistently Grow Marketshare From Within* (New York: McGraw-Hill, 2007). That work, in turn, led to his collaboration with Jeanne in which they created the Darden Growth Model and he further developed his concepts of Growth Systems and Growth Portfolios. He followed that work with a multidisciplinary research project looking for the empirical basis of the commonly held beliefs about business growth. Those research findings—"The Myths of Growth"—were published in his book *Smart Growth: Building an Enduring Business by Managing the Risks of Growth* (New York: Columbia University Press, 2010). In his private company research, Ed looked at the challenges faced by 54 high-growth private companies and has published those findings in two books, *Growing an Entrepreneurial Business: Concepts and Cases* (Stanford: Stanford University Press, 2011) and *Grow to Greatness: Smart Growth for Entrepreneurial Businesses* (Stanford: Stanford University Press, 2012).

Jeanne Liedtka

As a former consultant with BCG and then Strategy faculty member at the Darden Graduate School of Business at the University of Virginia, Jeanne struggled with how to help the managers she taught develop a skill set around producing organic growth. The scant academic research she found offered little in the way of insights—and even less in the way of tools. The traditional strategy frameworks taught to MBAs—SWOT analysis, 5 Forces, competitor analysis—didn't seem to be very helpful in locating and exploiting new growth opportunities. And the leadership literature was no better—despite a torrent of work talking about "good leadership," no one seemed to be even asking (much less answering) the obvious question: Was good *growth* leadership the same as just plain good leadership? With the support of Darden's Batten Institute, Jeanne and several of her colleagues set out to explore how great growth leaders acted and who they were. Over a period of three years, they interviewed and assessed the personality and practices of more than 60 managers singled out for their ability to produce better-than-market growth in mature organizations. They published their findings in *The Catalyst: How You Can Become an Extraordinary Growth Leader*, with coauthors Robert Rosen and Robert Wiltbank (New York: Crown Business, 2009). What they learned astonished them: much of what managers were being taught, while appropriate for their roles in leading in stable and predictable environments, was just plain *wrong* when it came to succeeding at growth.

Made in the USA
San Bernardino, CA
19 July 2017